Robert Grant

A Romantic Young Lady

Robert Grant

A Romantic Young Lady

ISBN/EAN: 9783744664844

Printed in Europe, USA, Canada, Australia, Japan

Cover: Foto ©Thomas Meinert / pixelio.de

More available books at **www.hansebooks.com**

"*Mr. Grant is nothing if not entertaining — nothing if not subtle. Himself a clever analyst, he defies analysis.*"
— THE UNIVERSITY.

MR. GRANT'S NOVELS.

THE KNAVE OF HEARTS.
1 vol. 12mo. $1.50.

"It is a companion to 'The Confessions of a Frivolous Girl,' being the autobiography of a young man who devotes himself to the profession of heart-breaking. The various species of American female flirts are amusingly and clearly sketched by a few light but powerful strokes, and this, together with the simple yet surprisingly successful methods employed to make the girls' acquaintance, to lead them gently on to the brink of the precipice, and then to drop them, instantaneously and utterly, makes the book a veritable 'flirt's vade mecum.'" — *The Argonaut.*

AN AVERAGE MAN.
1 vol. 12mo. $1.50.

"There is a good strong purpose throughout the story. The style is rapid and bright." — *Life.*

THE CONFESSIONS OF A FRIVOLOUS GIRL.
1 vol. 16mo. $1.25.

"The greatest social literary hit of the year." — *Chicago Tribune.*

"A screaming success." — *Saturday Review.*

"Clever and piquant sketches — refreshing spirit and vivacity." — *Harper's Magazine.*

A ROMANTIC YOUNG LADY.
1 vol. 12mo. $1.50.

Mr. Grant's latest work, and in many respects his best.

Sold by booksellers. Sent, postpaid, on receipt of price by the publishers,

TICKNOR & COMPANY, BOSTON.

BOSTON
TICKNOR AND COMPANY
211 Tremont Street

University Press:
JOHN WILSON AND SON, CAMBRIDGE.

A ROMANTIC YOUNG LADY.

I.

MY mother died in giving me birth. My father was a very rich man, a railway magnate, so called, absorbed in great business enterprises. Thus it happened that I was brought up between two fires, — my father's sister, Aunt Agnes; and my mother's sister, Aunt Helen.

Aunt Agnes was prim but cultivated. She wrote for reviews and wore eye-glasses, and her library table was habitually littered with pamphlets and tomes. On the other hand, Aunt Helen was a neat, dapper little woman, who lived in a gem of a house and delighted in bric-à-brac and entertaining. They were both spinsters. Each of them passed one evening in every week with me. On Tuesdays I dined with Aunt Agnes, and on Fridays with Aunt Helen. Thus I was alone only two evenings out of seven, for on Sundays my father did not go to the Club.

From the age of ten until I was fifteen I attended a private school. I proved ambitious and quick at my books. Aunt Helen was anxious that I should be well grounded in the modern languages, while Aunt Agnes wished me to pursue what she styled "serious" studies. In my efforts to please them both I broke down in health. My father was the first to observe my pallid cheeks, and at the advice of a physician I was taken away from school. For nearly a year I was idle, save that I read at random in my father's library. Then my aunts for once put their heads together and insisted upon my having a governess. They told my father that the next three years were the most important in my life, and that the best way to foster my health was to find some judicious person to be my companion.

Aunt Helen was in favor of one who had youth and good spirits, but Aunt Agnes thought it important that a governess should inspire respect. I was not consulted, and my father declined to arbitrate between them. In the end, the favorite of Aunt Agnes was installed, through the chance discovery that the other applicant had been at one time on the stage.

Miss Jenks was a kind but sober disciplinarian of fifty. I was her pupil until I was eighteen; and though I was none the less lonely because of her companionship, I am in her debt to-day for the pains she took to systematize my heterogeneous acquirements and teach me the evils of superficiality. Her views of life were autumnal in tint, and her laugh was never hearty. She rarely conversed with me at length; but if I made inquiries concerning any matter of knowledge, I was sure to find a book or pamphlet on my desk the next day, with slips marking the valuable pages. She kept me so steadily employed during the hours I was not in bed or in the fresh air that I had no time for novel-reading, — a pastime I had indulged in formerly to a considerable extent. I thrived physically under this regimen, but I became silent and grave. Miss Jenks seemed constantly on her guard against undue enthusiasm, and abetted by her example I inclined to introspection and over conscientiousness. I picked up pins, and went out of my way to kick orange-peel from the sidewalk, on principle.

But apart from, or rather concurrent with, this sobriety of character I was a dreamer in secret, and delighted to give the rein to fancy. I liked to picture myself in some of the romantic situations of which I had read, and to build castles for the future. But all these imaginations were of a realistic order, as distinguished from ghosts and fairies and other creations of that class. I was completely free from superstitions. It was not for luck that I picked up pins, but that they should not be wasted. In like manner I never hesitated to let a horse-shoe lie in the road, to walk under a ladder, or be one of thirteen at table. And yet I was distinctly a dreamer. If it was in the way of lovers, my thoughts were entirely subjective. I knew no young men except the boys at dancing-school; and they as a rule avoided me, for I was shy, and for the present only moderately pretty. I think I tried in my day-dreams to form an ideal of what a lover's mental and moral attributes should be without ever endowing the abstraction with a head. I found a happiness in doing so much, — akin, I fancy, to that of the votary who kneels before a shrine of which the doors are closed. It was the consciousness of a great possible happiness that thrilled me, rather than any definite vision.

When Miss Jenks left us I was a well educated girl for my age. What I knew I knew thoroughly, and the wishes of both my aunts had been respected. Perhaps the most striking circumstances connected with my bringing up, however, were that at eighteen I had no idea I was the heiress to an enormous fortune, and that I could pass young men in the street without self-consciousness. Strangely, too, I had grown up without having formed an intimacy with any girls of my own age. I have never quite been able to decide whether the ability I thus acquired to think for and by myself was more valuable than the happiness that results from such friendships; yet I have never distinctly regretted not having made a confidant among my contemporaries.

II.

MISS JENKS went away in October, and a few days later Aunt Helen broached the subject of preparations for the winter. I was to go into society; and she had taken upon her shoulders the burden of having me well-dressed and "presentable," as she called it. My clothes ordered from Paris were at her house, and she took even more pleasure than I in studying their effect when tried on, and in selecting from my mother's jewelry the most appropriate articles for my toilet. There were certain trinkets among them which she told me were all the rage; and she concluded with a homily that I was very fortunate to be able to have such expensive things to wear, and that many girls had to be content with two ball-dresses, or in some instances with one. I was glad to put myself entirely in her hands, for I felt that she knew about such matters. My own sensations were a mixture of timidity, bewilderment, and exultation.

One evening a short time previous to the beginning of the gay season my father turned to me and said, —

"There is something I wish to tell you, Virginia. I have recently made my will. With the exception of a few legacies for charitable uses and a bequest to each of your aunts, I have left everything to you. Very likely it may be a surprise to you to hear that you will be very rich. It is proper and right you should know it now, just as it was important you should remain in ignorance of the fact during childhood. I have requested hitherto your aunts and your governess to make no allusions to your future prospects. If I am not mistaken, you learn the truth from me for the first time."

He paused as if expecting an answer.

"Yes, it has never occurred to me to inquire about the future," said I. "I knew that we lived in comfort. Beyond that I have not thought on the subject."

"It is as I supposed," said my father. "Unless I see reason to alter the present distribution of my property, you will be one of the richest women in town. When you were a child, Virginia, I felt badly at times that you were not a boy; I wanted a son to inherit my name and fortune. But one day it occurred to me, that, though a daughter could not make money, she might learn to spend it as well as a son. The thought comforted me; for I have made all the money we can need for many generations to come, and my only desire is that when I am gone there shall be some one to use it as I would like. There is an idea, I know, that women are not fitted to comprehend the value of money, and that it is unwise to give them the control of large sums. However correct that may be, the tendency of all modern legislation shows that the world is in favor of their administering their own affairs. At any rate, I propose to make the experiment. Unless you convince me beforehand that I am mistaken, I shall leave you at my death the mistress of over three million dollars."

While I was trying to form a definite idea of so much wealth, my father rose, and going to a side-table took up a large tin box, on the top of which lay a plush-covered case and a pile of pamphlets.

"In this trunk," he said, "you will find one hundred thousand dollars in first-rate securities, registered in your name. I want you to learn, so far as is possible for a woman, the care of property. These newspapers and reports will help you somewhat. I shall be glad to answer all your questions, and will keep you supplied with the latest intelligence relating to your property; for I give you these stocks and bonds to use as you see fit. You will find a cheque-book and a bank-book inside. One must learn to appreciate the value of money in order to use it well. I would not advise you to change your investments at first without consulting me. You must expect to make mistakes at the outset, but I have great confidence in your good sense. I should have been afraid to make the experiment in the case of many girls."

These words of my father brought the tears to my eyes. He had been watching me after all, while I sometimes half fancied him oblivious of my existence. At the moment, I was too confused to do more than thank him and gather up in a dazed way the pamphlets he placed before me. He put the little key that dangled from the tin box into the lock, and disclosed to me the parchment securities within.

"Carefully managed, that ought to yield you six per cent net," said he.

"But what am I to do with so much money every year?" I cried aghast.

My father laughed, and said: "That is for you to decide, Virginia. You will learn only too soon the part that money plays in the world," he added gravely. "Prepare yourself to be courted and flattered for its sake. Some people would say, 'Do not destroy her faith in human nature. She will learn the truth soon enough.' I believe that to be forewarned is to be forearmed. Good and true men are abundant, but there are unscrupulous and mercenary ones as well, who will woo you for the sake of your fortune and not because they love you.

"One word more," said he, without regard to the expression of pain that overspread my face at his last speech. "Do not be afraid to use your money. Avoid foolish extravagance, but learn to enjoy life and the blessings at your disposal. It used to be considered wrong by our forefathers to surround themselves with beautiful things, and any but the simplest comforts. Some people are of that opinion still, but I do not agree with them. Your own good sense will be the best criterion of what is unduly ostentatious; but never hesitate to have anything you may wish because you fear the verdict of others. In short, be independent, and think for yourself if you wish to be happy. Your Aunt

Helen has undertaken the charge of your wardrobe; that is something of which I know nothing. I can tell when a young lady is well dressed, but I am not capable of selecting her dresses. Here, however," he said, taking the plush-covered case from the table, "is something that will make your toilet more complete."

I started with delight on raising the lid, to discover a superb necklace of the largest pearls. Under the impulse of the moment I flung my arms about my father's neck and kissed him. He seemed touched by my impetuosity, and stood for a moment with my head between his hands looking into my eyes.

"I believe you have in you the making of a noble woman, my dear," he said proudly. "You have your mother's sweet disposition, and also I think my fixity of purpose."

I lay awake that night for hours. It seemed to me that I had grown five years older in a single day, and I felt a new responsibility in living. My father's trust and generosity had stirred me deeply, and I made many a solemn vow not to prove unworthy of such confidence. But athwart the satisfaction these thoughts inspired, rose the recollection of what he had said regarding the insincerity of men. I had of course read in novels of fortune-hunters, but no suspicion of their existence within the pale of the polite society of which I was so soon to form a part had ever marred the rosy simplicity of my imagination. This was my first peep at the world's wickedness, and it shocked me to think that human nature could be so base.

I had seen but little of my Aunt Agnes during the autumn, perhaps because I more than half suspected she did not sympathize with the plans and preparations for my social education. I remembered some years before, at the time when the question of my attending dancing-school was being debated, to have heard her express disapproval of girls who frittered away their time and health in the pursuit of what she called "vain pleasures." I had not conversed with her on the subject, but I had obtained an intimation from her short and acrid manner on the one or two occasions when we had met of late that she was quite aware of what was going on, and condemned it unequivocally.

Although I knew that Aunt Agnes was very fond of me, and I in turn loved and respected her, she was apt to inspire me with awe even on ordinary occasions. Her character was as upright as her figure, which in defiance of the relaxed customs of the day was always arrayed against a straight-backed chair. Conventionalities of every sort were an abomination to her. Black silk was the full extent of her condescension in the matter of what she was pleased to call Babylonian attire, and she had no patience with the ordinary vanities of her sex.

She received me frostily when I went to visit her a few days after the conversation with my father, and suffered me to kiss both her cheeks in turn without evincing a sign of being mollified. Remembering that she was fond of directness, I opened fire at once by observing that I was invited to a ball at Mrs. Dale's a week hence.

"All girls are fools," she answered abruptly, after a moment. I bowed my head submissively, and awaited the storm.

"I expected better things of you, Virginia," she continued. "I hoped you were too sensible to follow the herd, and waste the best years of your life in folly."

"Folly?" I echoed faintly.

"Yes, folly. What else is it but folly to sit up night after night, until the small hours of the morning, waltzing with brainless young men?"

"But, Aunty, my father wishes me to go into society."

"Pshaw! What does he know about balls and parties? He is under the thumb of your Aunt Helen. At your age he was working hard for his living, and learning to be of use in the world."

"But I have not to earn my living," said I.

"So much the worse for you. Humph! You have found that out, have you?"

I understood that she referred to what my father had told me. "Yes, I know my father is very rich. If I do not go to parties, how am I to learn anything about life?"

"Life! You are very simple, child, if you expect to learn what life is by dancing the German. The first thing we shall hear is, that you are engaged to some young dandy who is after your fortune. Then you will be snuffed out. You will become a fashionable simpleton, who goes to bed at four and gets up at noon. Life, indeed!"

This cruel insinuation, following so soon upon what I had lately heard, cut like a knife. I answered firmly, —

"My father has already warned me to be on my guard against insincere persons."

"Much good a warning would do, if you were to take it into your head to like anybody! Tell *me!* I may not understand girls" (this was a thrust at Aunt Helen), " but I know the dispositions of my own family. When a Harlan gets a fixed idea, it takes a deal of pounding to drive it out; and you're a Harlan, Virginia, if there ever was one."

This last reflection seemed to console her a little, or at least to suggest the futility of trying to alter my determination; for after speaking of other matters for a few moments she exclaimed, —

"Well! girls will be girls, I suppose, to the end of time," — and rising she went to an escritoire and took out a small parcel, which it was evident she had intended to present to me from the first. "There, Virginia, if you are bent on being frivolous, is a bit of old lace that your Aunt Helen, or anybody else, would have to hunt a long time to equal. You will find a locket inside which I wore when your father was married. I shall never use such frippery again, and you might as well have them now as when I am dead."

Knowing that she meant to be gracious, I thanked her warmly. But having doubts regarding her taste, I abstained from opening the package until I reached home. Then I found that the lace even surpassed in exquisiteness the estimate Aunt Agnes had put upon it. Aunt Helen was fairly envious, and spent the evening in wondering "where on earth" her rival could have come into possession of such a treasure.

But the locket — a cameo, bizarre, and out of the run of ordinary personal ornaments — excited her contempt.

"It is fit for a woman of forty, and would make you look like a guy, Virginia."

The idea of looking different from other people did not disturb me. Indeed, I had resolved to be thoroughly independent. So, on the evening of Mrs. Dale's ball, I announced my intention of wearing the locket, and of reserving my necklace of pearls for some more brilliant occasion. Aunt Helen, who supervised my toilet, was greatly distressed at my obstinacy. Nevertheless I left the house with it on. But at the last moment my courage failed me; I slipped it off and put it in my pocket, — thus making a courtesy to conventionality on the threshold of society.

III.

MY recollections of the first few parties I attended are confused. A great many young men were introduced to me, but I scarcely distinguished one from another. I was alternately dazed and dazzled by the attentions I received. There is no object in disguising the fact that I had become very handsome, and my brilliant financial prospects were of course well known.

My emotions were doubtless those of an average society belle, eager to drain the cup of pleasure to the dregs. I lived to dance, and cared little with whom I danced, provided he danced well. The mere physical satisfaction of waltzing, coupled with the glamor of a universal homage, contented me.

But this did not last long. I learned to make distinctions, and to generalize; and from this primary stage of development I began to entertain positive likes and dislikes.

It was not however until the winter was waning that Mr. Roger Dale occupied a different place in my thoughts from half-a-dozen others, although he had been polite to me from the time of my first ball at his mother's house. It would be difficult to say exactly what distinguished him from the rest of their admirers in the eyes of every girl with any pretensions to beauty or style; but he was undeniably considered at that time, in the circle of my acquaintance, as the most fascinating man in society. He was commonly spoken of as interesting, and there was a vague impression that he was lacking in constancy. It was not unnatural therefore that I should be flattered at his singling me out for assiduous attentions, especially when he possessed the art of letting me understand in a quiet, gentlemanly fashion, and without the aid of garish compliments, that I was the only girl in the room for whom he cared a straw. I did not believe him, but I was pleased, for that was the way in which I wished to be wooed by the one whom I wished to believe.

So in course of time I became willing to retire with him into conservatories and ante-rooms to avoid interruption. I was still fond of dancing, but I had recovered from the frenzy which blinded me to everything but the rapture of the moment. I liked to hear Mr. Dale talk, and without an affinity of ideas our intimacy must have died a natural death. But we found a common ground of sympathy in our revolt against the subserviency in modern life of romance to matter-of-fact considerations. He harped upon this string, and awoke a corresponding chord in my breast. His ideas were a correlation of the dreams of my girlhood. I felt that I was understood. There was such a thing as the love I had imagined; Mr. Dale had pondered over it, fathomed it, and could talk about it. Not that I considered myself in love with him, or him with me. We simply were friends, — that was all. But existence seemed nobler when illumined by his theories.

He declared that the Puritan fathers and their descendants lacked the power of expression. People were afraid to acknowledge they loved. The ardor that distinguished the passion of other races and made it beautiful was nowhere to be found, for if it ever dared to manifest itself the breath of ridicule wilted its growth. The expensive " floral offering " was more prized than the single dewy bud of the true lover, and the zeal and sentiment of chivalry had yielded to the blighting prose of a commercial age.

My Aunt Helen was the first of the family to comment on my intimacy with him.

"What does your friend Mr. Dale do?" she asked one day.

"Do?"

"Yes. I mean what is his business down town?"

"I don't know, Aunt Helen," I answered; and I spoke the truth. I had never thought to inquire.

"The Dale blood is not the very best in the world," she continued presently, with her head bent over her work almost as though soliloquizing. "As regards position they are well enough, but two of this young man's uncles were extremely dissipated, and I fancy that the father was not much to boast of. He died early, just after I was grown up. I remember him though. He was a handsome creature."

I listened with glowing cheeks, but made no response.

"They have very little to live on I imagine," she observed nearly five minutes later.

"Of whom are you speaking?" I inquired with dignity.

"The Dales, child, of course. It was generally supposed that Mrs. Dale was left very poorly off. I believe her husband's life was insured for something, and they own their house. Pussy always looks well dressed, but they must have to scrimp in other ways."

Pussy Dale was Roger's eldest sister, a girl of just my age. They were a family of five, four of whom were daughters.

"I don't see that their being poor is anything against them," I said a little hotly.

"No-o," replied Aunt Helen reflectively, "perhaps not. But I don't know what your father would say to him for a son-in-law."

"A son-in-law? You have no right to make such insinuations, Aunt Helen," I protested. "Mr. Dale and I are friends, and nothing more."

"I am glad to hear it, dear; for though I should try to reconcile myself to whomever you chose, believing that a girl is the best judge of what will contribute to her own happiness, I own frankly that I should be better pleased with some one whose antecedents were a little more creditable."

I gritted my teeth and sewed industriously in silence for the rest of the evening. I felt injured, without scarcely knowing why. Aunt Helen's accusations were vague at best. It was impossible for me to doubt Mr. Dale. But on the other hand the idea of our marriage was not a serious consideration. Still I felt annoyed and troubled, and I could not help thinking of what my father and Aunt Agnes had said by way of warning. But though I lay awake long that night I fell asleep at last, convinced that Roger Dale was the noblest and sincerest soul alive, and that to doubt him would be to wrong the sacred name of friendship.

This conversation took place in March; but in the next two months Mr. Dale was so much at our house that I was not surprised when my father asked one evening the same question put to me by Aunt Helen. Our intimacy had continued without further developments, except a constantly increasing devotion on his part and a corresponding pleasure in his society on my own. I did not make my infatuation conspicuous by walking with him in the streets, but otherwise I did not attempt to disguise the partiality I felt for him. Had I mixed more with other girls before entering society I might have been less guileless. But as it was, I never thought of tempering by coquetry the satisfaction visible in my face whenever Mr. Dale appeared.

This time I was prepared with an answer to the question concerning his occupation down town: —

"He is in the wool business, and doing very well."

"A wool broker?"

"I think so."

"Humph!"

My father walked up and down the room a few times. "I have already cautioned you, Virginia, against false prophets who come to you in sheep's clothing."

He was jocose doubtless so as to pass the matter off lightly, and to spare my feelings. But I chose to be offended, and answered haughtily,—

"I don't understand what you mean."

He stood still and looked directly at me. "Simply this, Virginia: I trust you are too sensible to throw yourself away on a man who is not worthy of you."

"You do Mr. Dale a great injustice," I replied, with an assumption of dignity; "and me too." Whereupon I swept out of the room.

I flung myself upon my bed and burst into tears. These remarks of my father and aunt were straws, but they showed me how the wind was likely to blow. Those upon whom I had a right to rely for sympathy were ready to desert me first of all. It was cruel and unkind. Had I asked to be allowed to marry Mr. Dale? Had either of us ever hinted at the subject? Never! And yet my father was the first to cast suspicions and make insinuations, for I understood his unjust taunt. Sheep's clothing, indeed! Detraction was the surest way to make me love him; for if there was any one under the sun whose sentiments were noble and unselfish, whose motives were manly and disinterested, I believed it was Roger Dale. Why had my father spoken in such high terms of my good sense only six months ago if he thought it necessary to caution me again to-day? I felt bitter and wronged.

Just then my glance chanced to fall on the tin box in which were the securities my father had given me in the autumn, and I blushed as I reflected that except to deposit the dividends that were sent to me I had done nothing toward understanding the care of my property. I had used the cheque-book to give a little money in charity and to pay some bills, but the pile of financial pamphlets lay on the shelf of my desk still unread. I had not had time to devote myself to them, or rather the time had slipped away before I realized it.

There was some ground after all for my father's reproof. It was possible that my neglect and apparent disregard of his wishes had led him to speak severely of Mr. Dale. The thought comforted me and brought sleep to my eyes. I rose early, and spent an hour before breakfast in reading the Annual Report of one of the Railway Companies in which I held stock; and I went downstairs with a confused mind, but with a sense of awakened virtue. I was cheerful and animated at table, and asked several questions concerning mortgage bonds and sinking funds that brought a pleasant expression to my father's face.

The reason why I felt so buoyant was not merely the light-heartedness of repentance. My romantic spirit had conceived a scheme for convincing my father that he had unjustly sneered at Mr. Dale's business capacity. I was resolved to consult him as to my investments, and I felt sure that the profits accruing from his sage advice would plead his cause more eloquently than any words of mine. Let but my father perceive my admirer's sterling qualities, and I knew that he would be eager to make amends for his injustice by pushing him forward in business. The idea took strong possession of me, for ever since hearing Aunt Helen speak of Mr. Dale's lack of means I had been eager at heart to assist him. I would gladly have asked him to put my money into some commercial venture, and have insisted upon his keeping a portion of the gains; but to that I felt he would never consent.

And yet I did not believe that I was in love with Roger Dale. The thought never occurred to me. I was ready to have our relations continue indefinitely as they were. But I was not able to regard the hostility of my family without impatience that added a spice of martyrdom to my interviews with him. The very fact that others thought ill made it all the more incumbent upon me to be steadfast and undoubting.

IV.

BEFORE I had an opportunity to broach the question of investments to Mr. Dale, Aunt Agnes added her quota to my sense of wrong. One evening when she came to dinner I divined, from the intense rigidity of her posture at table, that she was offended with me. To tell the truth, I felt a trifle guilty. My visits to her during the winter had been spasmodic and hurried. What was worse, so greatly was I carried away by my social success, that whenever we did meet I prattled on about fashionable frivolities regardless of her frown. But though I was conscious of not standing in her good graces, I felt tolerably secure from comments on the score of Mr. Dale, for the reason that as she never went anywhere she would know nothing of my intimacy with him unless Aunt Helen or my father were to make her a confidant; and this I did not think likely. Therefore, when she introduced the subject while we were alone together in the drawing-room after dinner, I was a little disconcerted.

"Who is this Mr. Gale whose name I see connected with yours?" she asked severely.

"With mine?"

"Yes, with yours. Don't beat about the bush! You know perfectly well whom I mean."

"Excuse me, Aunt Agnes, there is no Mr. Gale among my acquaintance. I know a Mr. Dale."

She frowned, and began to fumble in her pocket. "The principle is the same whether it is Gale or Dale or Tompkins. I never expected to learn of my niece's engagement from the public press. I am confident the notice said 'Gale.' Ah! I thought so. Plain as the nose on your face," she added, producing from her porte-monnaie a newspaper cutting and reading aloud: "'It is rumored that the engagement of the beautiful and accomplished daughter of Augustus Harlan, the Railway Magnate, to Mr. Roger Gale of this city will soon be announced.'"

"It is not true, Aunt Agnes," I cried indignantly. Needless to say I was startled at this bit of information, coming too as it did from such an unexpected source. My aunt's knowledge of it seemed fully as remarkable to me as the fact of the publication.

"I trust not," she replied with emphasis. "I did not seriously suppose my own niece so far lost to all sense of propriety as to take such a step unbeknown to me. But it seems to me, Virginia, you must have been behaving in a, to say the least, very peculiar manner, to get your name into the newspapers. Where there is so much smoke there is apt to be a little fire. Who is this Mr. Gale?"

"His name is Dale, Aunt Agnes."

"Well, Dale then. You won't put me off by quibbling. If you want your father to know of it, you are taking just the course to make me tell him."

"My father knows all there is to know. Mr. Dale is a friend of mine and comes to the house by permission. There is no possibility of an engagement between us."

"An engagement! I should hope not. Do you consider yourself qualified to enter upon the cares and responsibilities of married life?"

"I have already said that I have no intention of getting married."

"Getting married! Why, the child is crazy. You talk of matrimony as if it were as simple a proceeding as changing your dress or going to a party."

"Some people would appear to find it so," I answered, goaded to impertinence.

But Aunt Agnes apparently did not perceive my innuendo. "I dare say," said she with asperity. "That is because there are so many fools in the world."

We sat in silence for some minutes. My aunt was so much excited that I could see her hands tremble as she put the obnoxious cutting back into her porte-monnaie. All of a sudden she looked at me over her glasses and said, —

"I am willing to give you one more chance, Virginia."

I waited for her to continue.

"If you choose to take advantage of it, well and good. If not, you must go your own ways. I am not going to make my life a burden over you any longer. If you prefer to be giddy and foolish, let those take the responsibility who have encouraged you to become so. No one shall blame me."

"You know, Aunt Agnes, I wish to be nothing of the sort."

"Very well, then. I propose to pass the summer in Europe, and it strikes me as an excellent opportunity for you to cut adrift from the objectionable associations you have formed during the past few months. With a fresh start, and surroundings calculated to inspire in you a desire for self-improvement, it will not be too late to hope for better things. I have every confidence in the natural stability of your character if you are once put upon the right track. I blame your advisers more than I blame you."

I listened to her words with some disquietude. I had never crossed the Atlantic, and at any ordinary time would have jumped at the chance. But I had already other plans in store for the summer that I did not feel prepared to relinquish, even for the pleasure of a trip to Europe.

"It is very kind of you to think of me," I said.

"No, it isn't. It's only natural," she answered shortly. "You are my brother's child, and let alone any affection I may have for you, it is my duty to save you from harm if I can."

"Who else is going?" I asked out of sheer cowardice; for I had already made up my mind to decline the invitation.

"Who else? Nobody. If a woman at my age has not learned to travel without an escort, it is time she did. I suppose that's what you're driving at. Well, what do you say? Go, or remain at home as you like. Only I shall regard it as a choice once and for all."

"Aunt Agnes," I answered with an endeavor to express in my tone and manner the affection and gratitude I felt, "I thank you with all my heart for your kindness. Whatever you may say, it *was* extremely kind of you to offer to take me abroad with you, and I wish I could go."

"What is there to prevent your going?" she inquired sharply.

I hesitated an instant, and then boldly spoke the truth, though I knew it would operate like a two-edged sword: —

"I have already promised to spend the summer at Tinker's Reach with Aunt Helen, and she would be disappointed if I failed her at the last moment, for all her plans are made on that understanding."

"Ah! That is it," she replied with bitter calmness.' "Very well, I disclaim all further responsibility. You act with your eyes open, and must take the consequences."

There was so much pain and concern in her expression that for an instant I hesitated, and thought of changing my mind. I went to her and knelt down beside her chair.

"Aunt Agnes, you must not talk so. I love you as dearly as I love Aunt Helen; and if I had not promised to spend the summer with her I should be delighted to go with you. Do not repulse me. I have so few relatives to care for me, and I shall be very unhappy if you go away angry."

But she refused to be mollified. She did not scold me, and she coldly suffered me to embrace her at parting; but her air was more grim than I had ever seen it, and I was conscious of having wounded her deeply.

Perhaps it is needless to say that Mr. Dale was at the bottom of my decision. A few weeks previous I had confided to him that Aunt Helen had invited me to spend the summer with her at her new cottage at Tinker's Reach. He assured me that there were few more charming spots, that it was a favorite resort of his own, and that he himself proposed to pass his vacation there. Naturally, I felt bound to a certain extent after this to go to Tinker's Reach. Indeed, I was eagerly looking forward to a continuance of our friendship under such happy auspices.

When I had spoken to Mr. Dale regarding his business he replied, as I have already stated, that it was "wool." But I noticed he was brief, and his manner did not encourage me to ask further questions. I ascribed his reserve to modesty, or the proper reluctance some people have to talk of private affairs that in no way concern the interrogator. This impression was heightened by the investigations which I quietly made in regard to the point, feeling that though I could not admit the possibility of a doubt even in regard to his business sagacity, it was well to have evidence with which to rebut the insinuations of my family. Every one of the young men whom I questioned regarding Mr. Dale's prospects assured me that he was doing very well, and attended his office daily.

This was pleasant tidings, and encouraged me to speak to him of the matter I had at heart. With all my tendency to romance and indifference to the opinion of others, I realized that it must be delicately handled. I must not seem to offer a gift or to place him under an obligation. Accordingly, one day shortly before we left town, I explained to him the condition of my affairs; how my father had settled a sum upon me with the request that I should manage it intelligently, with a view to having the control of larger amounts later. I said further that I was anxious to learn, and to acquit myself with credit; and that it had struck me as a brilliant scheme to double my property (I fixed upon this as a reasonable estimate) by some investment. He listened to my words with close attention, and as he made no comment at this point I said: —

"You are down town, Mr. Dale, and must necessarily understand business matters. I come to you for advice. I want you to tell me what to buy. I will give you the money, and when you think it time to sell I will authorize you to do so. You see I am not entirely ignorant myself."

Roger Dale gave a short laugh, and made no response for a moment. "It wouldn't do," he said at last, shaking his head. "What would your father say if he heard of it? He doesn't have any too high an opinion of me already, I fancy."

"But, Mr. Dale, that would be the very way to prove to him that you are a practical business man. If my father were to take you into his confidence he could push you ahead very fast, I know. I will show him the profits of your investments, and bestow the credit where it belongs."

The idea seemed to amuse him, for he laughed again. "You seem to forget, Miss Harlan, that instead of profits you might lose it all."

"That would be impossible. I have too much confidence in your judgment to fear any such result," I answered sweetly, led away by the eagerness I felt to obtain his consent to the project.

He gave me a swift sidelong glance that made me tremble and set my heart fluttering, though I did not know why.

"Besides," I said speaking fast and feverishly, "the money is mine. I have a right to do what I please with it."

There was a pause, and then he said with the same glance, only longer and intenser than before: "Miss Harlan, I cannot accept such a responsibility unless you give it to me forever."

I was stunned. I had brought this upon myself I could see plainly, now that it was too late. My undignified, unfeminine conduct stood out before me the moment he had spoken, in all its mortifying nakedness. He had mistaken my meaning, but it was I who was to blame for the error. Humiliated and confused, I was at a loss for words; but a reply was necessary.

"You have misunderstood me entirely, Mr. Dale. Let us change the subject, if you please," I said with dignity.

Fortunately some one came in just at this moment, and Mr. Dale shortly rose to go. But he dared in taking leave to look at me again in the manner I have described, and in spite of my will and desire my eyes fell as they encountered his.

We did not meet again, much to my relief, before I left town. I was in an harassing state of mind, and happiness alternated in my thoughts with despair. For a terrible secret had dawned upon me, — terrible, because I foresaw the painful consequences which would result therefrom. I loved Roger Dale. It was useless to disguise it longer from myself. His words had made the truth manifest, and that which I fancied friendship was become a mutual passion. Any mortification I may have felt at having unwittingly prompted the speech that had filled my heart with joy was nullified by the consciousness that I was beloved.

But the thought of braving the opposition of my family distressed me beyond measure, as it must needs distress any conscientious girl in a similar position. My instincts told me that it was vain to hope that they would relent. Their objections were baseless, but none the less I knew that they would prove insuperable. I found myself face to face with a dilemma fraught with unhappiness whichever way I should solve it. What was there to allege against Mr. Dale? Nothing. He was poor. But what of that? My father had money enough for us both. Why need he mar by cruel suspicions and prejudices this great joy of my life? I remember to have wondered sometimes that girls could marry contrary to the consent of their parents, but it seemed to me now that no one could sacrifice an attachment as strong as mine to blind authority without doing wrong to the eternal principles of love and honor. I vowed in secret that if Roger Dale should prove as true to me as I would be to him, nothing should keep us apart.

V.

TINKER'S REACH, as most people know, is a very popular summer resort on the Atlantic sea-coast. It possesses the advantages both of the ocean and the country. There are beautiful drives in its vicinity variegated by mountain peaks, ponds almost large enough to be classed as lakes, and extensive woods where one — or more readily two — may be lost with ease. On the other hand the harbor is adapted to all sorts of craft, from the two hundred ton yacht to the bark canoe; and for those who prefer looking at the waves to riding over them, there are superb rocks to sit upon and clamber over, which abound in eyries for the retiring and caves for the curious. Altogether it is a delightful place.

It takes its name, not as might be supposed from one of the aborigines, but from a small variety of mackerel known to fishermen as "tinkers," which used to be seined off the main head-land in large quantities. Originally a primitive settlement, fashionable patronage had dotted the shore with large hotels and showy villas, which at this period were less numerous than at present.

Soon after my arrival I received a note from Mr. Dale announcing that he would be able to get away from the city by the end of the week. The receipt of this missive thrilled me with joy; but I felt that proper sentiments obliged me to tell my Aunt Helen. It would scarcely be honorable to carry on an affair of which she disapproved, while enjoying her hospitality and under her protection. Besides, I was not without hopes of winning her over to my side. She had always been the one to whom I had gone for sympathy, and her desertion in this case made me feel sadly the need of an ally. So I said to her one evening, —

" Mr. Dale will be here early next week."

Aunt Helen shifted uneasily in her chair. " I don't know what your father would say to that. He disapproves of your intimacy with Mr. Dale."

"I know it, Aunt Helen. He is prejudiced against him."

" Mr. Dale is certainly a very constant young man," she replied.

My heart gave a bound. Her remarks before

had been rather in the form of criticisms than regular objections. I laid down my work with the resolve to throw myself on her mercy.

"Aunt Helen, why is it that all of you are so opposed to Mr. Dale?"

"Opposed! Well, dear, I should hardly call it that," said my aunt. "Your father has an idea, I believe, that Mr. Dale is mercenary in his views. What foundation for it he may have I do not know. As for myself, I cannot say I am opposed, for I scarcely know the young man."

"My father is very unjust," I said with tears in my eyes.

"It may be, dear. Very likely he would own himself that it was merely an impression; but it is only right that he should watch over your interests carefully."

"Is it watching over my interests to cast suspicion on the motives of one of my best friends?"

"It will all come right in the end, dear."

"He is noble and high-minded. No one shall say anything against him in my presence," I cried fiercely.

My aunt smoothed out the lap of her dress reflectively. "You are quite justified in standing up for your friend, Virginia. No one can blame you for that. I have no doubt this young Dale is all you describe him to be. Only," she added, with an apologetic cough, "be discreet. Some persons, perhaps, would wish to be better informed before ceasing to feel uneasy. I believe, though, in trusting to a girl's own instinct in these matters: it rarely goes astray. If my parents had followed that course, I might have been more happy."

She raised her handkerchief to her eyes to stay a tear, and with an impulse of gratitude and pity I went to her and kissed her.

"Yes," she murmured, acknowledging my sympathy with a pressure of the hand, "when I was just about your age there was a young man who was very fond of me, and I liked him. He wished to marry me."

"And your father objected to him?"

"He thought we were too young. He insisted upon our waiting until we had more money. So we did, and he fell into bad habits, and — and we drifted apart. It is a long story."

"Oh, Aunt Helen, I am very sorry."

"Thank you, dear. I should never have told you except to show that I could sympathize with you. Only, as I have said, be discreet. It is a serious responsibility for me to assume. I hope you will take no decisive steps without consulting your father Kiss me, Virginia."

We embraced with fervor, and I was sure that I had gained an ally.

Mr. Dale arrived on the expected day and was kindly welcomed by my aunt, who asked him to stay to tea. It was a superb evening, and he proposed that we should go out on the water as was the custom at Tinker's Reach.

He had been an accomplished oar in College, and a dozen strokes sent the light boat skimming beyond the bevy of similar craft by which we were surrounded. The sea was calm as a mill-pond, and the moon was at the full. I lay back with my face turned to the heavens and my fingers trailing in the cool water. Mr. Dale rowed on until the lights on shore seemed mere specks, and we could just perceive the gentle roll of the Atlantic swell. He rested on his oars and listened. The voices of the others were lost in the distance, and only the tinkle of a banjo wafted from afar broke the night's tranquillity. The water was alive with phosphorescence that sparkled like gems around the blades.

We had neither of us spoken since starting. I know not what were his thoughts, but mine were full of happiness. I felt sure, — sure of his love, and sure that he should have mine for the asking. And yet, so perfect was my peace, that I hoped he would postpone the words that were to make us still nearer to each other. We had talked so much of love and of its rapture and unselfishness earlier in our acquaintance, that now it was come to us silence seemed the most fitting commentary.

But he had made up his mind to speak at once.

"Virginia, I have brought you out here where we are alone, and where only Nature can interrupt us, to tell you that I adore you. Let the inconstant moon and twinkling stars laugh as they please. I know that true love exists, for my soul is full of it at this moment. Speak, dearest, and make me happy forever."

In the fulness of my transport at his ardent words, it seemed to me that heaven was come down to earth. My dreams had promised no such blessedness as this. Faintly and softly I murmured, —

" Roger, you know that I love you with all my heart."

" My darling!"

" My beloved!"

Is there an hour to compare in unqualified happiness with that in which a woman of impulsive nature, ignorant of the world and blindly trusting, whispers the confidences of her innocent bosom in the ear of her accepted lover? Roger and I, alternately silent with bliss or overflowing with the rapture of the heart's language, strolled arm in arm along the moonlit shores far into the night.

Only one incident marred our content. "Virginia," said Roger suddenly, "what will your father say?"

My father! I had never thought of him. So absorbing had been the consciousness that Roger Dale loved me and I returned his love, that every other consideration was blotted from my mind.

"Not to-night. We will not talk of that to-night. Let me be happy while I can," I cried, pressing his arm with feverish fondness.

"He dislikes me then? I was sure of it," he said quietly, but there was a scowl on his face.

"He does not know you, Roger. But I will make him give his consent. He cannot refuse me anything."

We walked on in silence. I felt stirred and rebellious. "Dearest," said I, in a low tone of determination, "I will be true to you whatever happens."

He stooped his head and kissed me. "If you are as constant to me, sweet Virginia, as I shall be to you, nothing can separate us."

Oh, joyous words! Were they not the very same with which I had fortified my courage scarcely a month ago?

We parted just after midnight. My aunt was sitting up for me, and I burst into the room in great excitement.

"Oh, Aunt Helen, I am engaged, I am engaged! I am so happy!"

"My darling child!"

We wept in each other's arms.

"He is so noble, Aunty; so good and kind!"

"God grant he may continue so!" she said, stroking my hair.

I gave a vent to my ecstasy in talk. While I rattled on she sat drying her eyes and looking at me with a half fond, half uneasy expression. Now and again she sobbed hysterically. At last she exclaimed, "What will your father say?"

"We will think of that to-morrow," I said. "I mean to be perfectly happy to-night."

"You will have to write to him of course."

"We have decided on nothing yet."

"Oh, Virginia, I am all in a flutter. What *will* he say? He is sure to blame me, and Heaven knows I acted for what seemed to me the best."

"It *was* the best, dear Aunt Helen. Can't you see how happy I am? When Roger and I are married, you shall come and live with us always, and have the best room in the house; for if it had n't been for you I might never have known what it is to be loved by the noblest man in the world."

It was a long time before I fell asleep. I was aroused in the morning by a knock at my door. It was Aunt Helen.

"Let me in," she said mysteriously.

"Well?" said I when I had risen and admitted her, "what is it? What has happened?"

"Your father has just arrived. He is downstairs."

"Father?"

"Yes. He knows nothing of course. I have scarcely slept a wink all night, Virginia. I feel dreadfully nervous. What *will* he say?"

I got back into bed and drew the clothes up to my chin in an affectation of composure. But I was overwhelmed by the news. His opposition seemed a much more serious consideration than when regarded by moonlight. A visit from him at any other time would not have been a surprise, for he had said he should run down to Tinker's Reach at his first leisure moment.

My aunt stood at the foot of the bed, watching my face and expecting me to speak.

"What do you mean to do about it?" she asked.

"Tell him," I replied.

"I suppose you might put it off until you return to town, especially if you would make up your mind to see very little of Mr. Dale in the mean time."

"No. It is best to have it over and done with. I want it settled now and forever." I felt my courage hardening.

"Well, Heaven bless you, child!" she said, kissing me. "You must admit, Virginia, that I have warned you all along that your father was opposed to Mr. Dale."

"It is not your fault in any way, Aunt Helen. I shall tell him so."

She left me, and I dressed deliberately. There was evidently no escape from the situation. But upon one point I was perfectly decided: nothing should induce me to give up Roger. I was ready to postpone our wedding for the present, or to humor my father's objections in any reasonable way. But renounce him, never! Having arrived at this determination I went downstairs. My father was eating his breakfast, and I waited until he was comfortably settled with a cigar on the sofa, before making my confession. Aunt Helen had taken the precaution to absent herself from the room. I began bravely: —

"Father, there is something I wish to tell you that interests me very deeply."

He removed the cigar, and looked at me inquiringly. I saw he did not suspect the truth.

"I am engaged to be married to Mr. Roger Dale. You must not be angry, father," I continued hastily. "You cannot help liking him when you know him better. He is worthy of me in every way."

I ventured to look at him; he was smoking with quick, nervous puffs that betokened great excitement.

"Bah!" he cried presently. "Bah! what a fool I have been! I might have known it would end in some such way as this. No girl ever had a better opportunity than you, and yet you are ready to sacrifice everything for the sake of a fellow who is no more fit to be your husband than the veriest beggar in the street. You have disappointed me terribly, Virginia. I believed you to be sensible and clever; but the admission you have just made proves you to be little short of a goose. Bah! you couldn't have chosen worse. A dissipated, mercenary good-for-nothing!"

"You must not speak in that way of Roger, father. I cannot sit here and let him be abused. Scold me as much as you please, but don't say anything against him. You do not understand him."

"Understand him, indeed! It is you who do not understand him. I never expected that a daughter of mine would fall in love with a barber's block."

This was too much for my endurance. "You are unjust," I cried with flashing eyes. "It is too late to talk so. We love each other, and if my own father repulses me we must go elsewhere for a blessing."

I have an idea that I looked like a queen of tragedy as I stood and braved him thus, for he gazed at me with a sort of astonishment, and made a movement as if to deter me from leaving the room. Just then, as fortune willed, the door was thrown open, and the servant ushered in Roger Dale.

He looked from the one to the other of us, and his cheeks reddened.

"So, sir," exclaimed my father, "you have come to claim your bride! You will have to reckon with me first; and I warn you that you will need stronger arguments than any I have ever heard in your favor, to convince me that you are the proper man to marry my daughter. Virginia, you may leave us. I will send for you when I wish for you. This gentleman and I are capable of settling this matter together."

I saw that my father was in a rage that would not brook resistance. But my own blood was boiling. Roger stood pale but seemingly unabashed, gazing at me as if he waited for me to speak. I addressed him: —

"Whatever my father may say to you, Roger, do not forget that I have promised to be your wife." With this speech I left the room.

VI.

I WENT to my room and bolted the door. Presently Aunt Helen knocked, but I declined to let her in. I felt grievously wronged. My father had trampled upon the most sacred sentiments of my soul. He had spurned and insulted the man I loved. What proofs had he of the charges he had brought? Dissipation! It could not be. I surely would have discovered this long ago if it had been true. Mercenary! Could he be called mercenary whom a high sense of honor had forbidden to assist me in the investment of my property? Good for nothing! Ah, my father did not know the noble impulses that underlay Roger Dale's unostentatious manner!

I do not know how long it was before Aunt Helen knocked a second time, and said that my father had sent for me. It was probably not more than half an hour, but it had seemed to me an eternity. I was waiting for the summons, with the box containing my securities beside me;

and with this in my hands I confronted my father once more in the parlor.

He was no longer visibly angry. Both he and Roger were smoking, and sitting at ease as I entered. I took a chair close by my lover's side, and looked at him fondly. He returned my glance, but there was a shadow of annoyance in his expression that made me feel uneasy. It brought to my mind his face as I had noticed it the previous evening, when he spoke of my father's prejudice against him.

At last my father saw fit to begin. He spoke in a deliberate, business-like tone, free from passion. "I have sent for you, Virginia, to repeat to you what I have already said to Mr. Dale. Once and for all, I will never give my consent to your marriage. I am utterly and radically opposed to it. I have been from the first, as you are aware. If you ask for my reasons, I do not consider this gentleman fitted to be my son-in-law. He has on his own admission no means to support a wife; he has no ambition or desire to excel, and I know from positive evidence that his habits are by no means exemplary."

He paused, and I glanced anxiously at Roger; but his eyes were fixed on the floor, and he sat drumming gently on the table with the fingers of one hand.

"If you persevere in this piece of folly contrary to my expressed wishes, you do it, Virginia, at your own peril, for I warn you that my resolution is fixed and cannot be shaken. Do not hope, either of you, by nursing the affair along to overcome my objections later. That is a favorite resort of young people in novels; but if fathers in real life are so weak in general, I shall prove an exception. As you know, Virginia, the part of a tyrannical parent is the last I ever expected to be called upon to play. I have allowed you every indulgence, and trusted you to an extent that I am beginning to believe was unwise. But I will not waste time in words; my resolution is perfectly explicit. My will is made in your favor. If I should die to-day, you would be mistress of all my property. Unless you promise me not to marry this man, I shall alter it to-morrow, and neither of you shall ever receive one cent from me during my lifetime or at my decease. This sounds like a threat, but it is only intended to show to the fullest extent in my power how fatal to your happiness I consider this union would be. I can say no more than this. I cannot prevent you from marrying Mr. Dale if you are bent upon it. There are no laws to punish foolish women or mercenary men; but you must take the consequences. What you have in that box," he continued, nodding towards me, "is all you will ever receive at my hands. If I am not mistaken, this young gentleman would play ducks-and-drakes with that in a very short time. I have said my say, and now you can suit yourselves."

I had listened to his words with a constantly increasing indignation that overshadowed the remorse I felt at having disappointed his hopes. So incensed was I at his aspersions of Roger that I almost laughed when he spoke of disinheriting me. But the taunt that Roger was courting me for my money was most galling of all, by very force of reiteration. I started to my feet once more with a defiant air.

"It is not true. You misjudge Mr. Dale cruelly. To show you, father, how free our love is from the base and paltry motives you impute, and that we do not need your help, see there!"

I rushed through the open window which led to the piazza, and before either my father or Roger divined my intention, hurled with all my might the box of securities over the railing into the sea beneath. It opened just before reaching the water, and the contents were submerged by the seething surf.

I re-entered the parlor with a triumphant air. Roger's face wore a half-scared look as he began to realize what I had done.

"Mad girl!" cried my father with a sneer. "Mr. Dale will not thank you for that, I fancy. You have, however, done me an infinite service." He turned and left the room.

When he was gone, exhausted and unnerved I buried my face on Roger's shoulder and sobbed bitterly. He tried to soothe me, and finally induced me to sit down. He sat beside me, holding my hand and urging me to calm myself. At last I turned to him and said with a sudden transport of new happiness, and smiling through my tears, —

"I promised to remain true to you, Roger, and I have."

"Yes, dear, I know. When you are a little more composed, we will talk the matter over seriously."

There was something in his tone that chilled me; he was so calm, and I so carried away by excitement.

"Do not think of my father's words," I said.

"Forget them. I shall be perfectly happy so long as you love me."

"He will never relent," he answered gloomily. "He is known down town as a man who makes up his mind once for all time."

"I would rather disobey my father than be false to you," I responded firmly.

"Yes. But how are we to live?" he asked, rising from the sofa and promenading the room nervously, with his hands in his pockets.

"Live?" I echoed.

"Unfortunately we should have to eat and drink, like everybody else. It was a pity," he continued reflectively, "that you flung that money overboard; we might have been very comfortable with that."

"Yes," I replied in a dazed sort of way.

"Was it the whole?" He stood looking at me with his head on one side.

"The whole of what?"

"Was all the property your father gave you in that box?"

"Certainly: I wonder you ask, Roger."

He walked up and down a few times and then took a seat beside me.

"Let us look at this matter in a common-sense way, Virginia. Heaven knows I love you, and that I am as romantic in my feelings as any one could desire. But suppose we were to marry without your father's consent, what would be the result? We should starve. To speak frankly, I find it difficult enough to make both ends meet as a single man. You are used to every luxury and comfort, and have not been accustomed to economize. Do not misunderstand me, Virginia," he continued, speaking quickly, struck perhaps by my expression, which if my emotions were adequately reflected therein must have made him uneasy. "I know that you are capable of any sacrifice; it is I who am unwilling to permit you to give up your fortune and your family for my sake. If there were any chance of your father's relenting, if I thought there was a possibility that time would make a difference in his views, I would not speak so. But as it is, I see no alternative for us but an unsuccessful struggle with poverty, that would end in unhappiness. It breaks my heart to come to this conclusion, but justice to you, as well as common-sense, will not let me suffer you to commit a folly which after the glamour of the moment was over, you would regret."

It was the manner even more than the matter of his speech that stabbed me to the heart.

Had he spoken less calmly and deliberately, I might have believed that he shrank from accepting my self-sacrifice, and have regarded his dampening words as a mere cloak for his own generosity. But his unconcerned and dispassionate air left no doubt in my mind that it was he who was unwilling to face the romantic but desperate circumstances in which my father's decree had placed us. Instinct told me that he in whose constancy and in whose devotion to ideality I had believed with all the ardor and trust of which I was capable, was false, and ready to subordinate a love like ours to temporal considerations.

Yet with the persistence of one who clutches at any semblance of hope however slender, I refused to believe the truth without further evidence.

"I should not be a burden to you, Roger. People can live on much less than they suppose. We could both work, I as well as you."

He shrugged his shoulders, and taking both my hands in his looked into my face with a trivial smile, so little in accord with the intensity of my feelings that I almost shrieked with pain.

"Do you think I would allow my dear girl to demean herself in any such way as that? No, no!

Love in a cottage is a delightful theory, but put into practice it becomes terribly disappointing."

I drew away my hands from him and sat for some moments in silence.

"I think it is best that our engagement should come to an end," I said presently.

He made a sigh of resignation. "That is for you to decide. It rests with you, of course."

"I agree with you that it would be very foolish of us to marry without my father's consent, Mr. Dale."

He drew himself up a little, and looked at me as if hurt. "Are you angry with me, Virginia?"

"Angry? Why should I be angry?"

"Then why call me Mr. Dale?"

"Because," I answered quietly and firmly, though I felt my anger rising, "unless you are to be my husband, you must be Mr. Dale."

"Can we not be friends?" he asked in a dejected tone.

"We can never be anything else," I answered with some ambiguity; and I rose and rang the bell.

The servant entered. "Tell Mr. Harlan, please, that I would like to speak to him."

"I think we are acting for the best," he said, after an awkward pause.

"I am sure we are, Mr. Dale." It was undignified, it may be, to betray my feelings, but my love was too strong to die without a murmur.

My father looked inquiringly at us as he entered. His face seemed to me almost haggard.

I said at once, "Father, we have made up our minds that you are right. It would be madness in us to marry without your consent. The credit of our decision belongs to Mr. Dale. He has proved to me that our engagement should come to an end."

My father turned toward him with a scornful smile, appreciating, I think, the gentle sarcasm of my words. But I doubt if Roger did, for he added immediately, —

"Yes, sir; I cannot consent to the sacrifice your daughter is prepared to make."

"I am glad that she as well as you have come to your senses, and I thank you for making the only amends possible for having endeavored to enter my family contrary to my desire, by teaching my daughter her duty. I have no doubt that we shall both be very grateful to you in the future."

This time Roger perceived that he was being laughed at, for his cheeks flushed. But he recovered his composure, and looking at me, said, —

"I trust I may continue to come to see you as usual."

I trembled all over at his words, but I controlled myself, and answered, —

"If you wish."

After a few moments of awkward hesitancy he left us.

When I knew that he was really gone, I could restrain myself no longer. Sinking into a chair, I covered my face with my hands and burst into a flood of tears. "Oh, father, he has deceived me! He has broken my heart!"

BOOK II.

SOPHISTICATION.

I.

IN the bitterness of my humiliation and distress at the perfidy of Roger Dale I came near running away from home. My youthful imaginations, as I have already mentioned, were of a realistic order, and it had been a favorite scheme with me to become a shop-girl. So when this sorrow overwhelmed me, I thought seriously of going out into the world to seek my fortune in some such capacity. It was only my father's kindness during those dreadful first days that deterred me from carrying out some romantic plan of escape. I felt sore and mortified, and ready to take any steps that would separate me from my old surroundings.

Aunt Helen did her best to comfort me, but I was in no frame of mind to talk it all over, which was, I knew, her main idea of solace, — that and frequent offers of tempting food. On the other hand, my father made no allusion to the wretched incident during the fortnight he remained at Tinker's Reach. He treated me exactly as if nothing had happened, except that every morning after breakfast he proposed a walk through the woods or up the mountain. Indifferent to everything as I was at the moment, I had a consciousness that this exercise was beneficial to me, and I was grateful at heart. Anything was better than harping over and over again on the same string the story of my wrongs. Walking interrupted this in a measure, though during the long tramps which I had with my father we rarely talked, and I usually in monosyllables. In this manner we explored the outlying country within a radius of twenty miles, and when night came I was so fatigued that I was apt to sleep, and consequently was spared the pale cheeks and dull eyes that for the most part afflict those who have undergone an experience similar to mine.

One of the reasons why I did not run away from home was my lack of funds. I was penniless, for all my money was with the securities I threw into the sea. I was inclined, however, to congratulate myself upon this extravagant proceeding, for the reason that had I acted less impulsively I might not have detected Roger's selfishness until it was too late. But when just before my father went away he handed me a roll of bank-bills, the color rose to my cheeks, and I began to reflect upon the enormity of my offence. He told me that he had ordered a saddle-horse to be sent to me from town, which he hoped I would use regularly, and that in the autumn he proposed to take me with him on a journey to California.

I listened in silence; but I rode the horse, and found him just the companion I required. He could not talk, and yet was sufficiently spirited to prevent me from self-absorption. My father also sent me a box of books, which embraced a variety of literature. Although there were some light and amusing sketches among them, novels of sentiment and poetry had been excluded. On the other hand he had picked out the latest and most authoritative publications relating to history, science, biography, and travel, by which I soon found myself engrossed and diverted. I read voluminously, and when this supply was exhausted I wrote home for more.

This was my interest during the remainder of the summer, and when autumn came I was conscious of having undergone a mental change. Whereas I was formerly trusting, credulous, and optimistic, at least toward all except myself, I was become suspicious even of the seal of sincerity, weighed words, and applied the scalpel of analysis to others' motives as well as to my own.

But this cynical phase did not last long, and gave way in turn to a much more serious view of life than I had hitherto taken. The trip which I made to California with my father did much to promote this. We were absent from home eight weeks, and we visited all the principal cities and saw the chief sights of the West. My father was assiduous in his kindness. He took pains to explain to me the immense value and importance of the wool and the wheat and the cattle and the ore which were the staple products of the States and Territories through which we passed. He showed me on the map the immense net-work of railways by means of which these industries, if not consumed at home, were carried to the seaboard either of the Atlantic or the Pacific, and made profitable to the producer by exportation to foreign lands. He tried to interest me in such commercial and economic questions, so that, as he said, I need not like most women remain in entire ignorance regarding the vital interests of the world. Although I was still stolid and indifferent in manner, I listened attentively to his instructions and appreciated the service he was doing me.

One evening shortly after our return, Aunt Helen said to me, with a prefatory cough which was apt to be a sign that she regarded the topic to be broached as delicate, —

"Virginia, it is time for you to be thinking about your party dresses. Of course it is too late now to send to Paris; but I fancy it is possible to get tolerable things here, if one is ready to pay a little more."

"I shall not require party dresses. I am not going anywhere this winter," I answered quietly.

As I have just intimated, Aunt Helen was somewhat apprehensive regarding my plans, owing to a few hints which I had let fall at Tinker's Reach. She had suggested my sending an order to Paris about a fortnight subsequent to my last interview with Mr. Dale, but I declined emphatically to do so. It was evident, however, from her expression that my resolve was a source of surprise and dismay to her.

"Not go anywhere? Why, people will think you are ill."

"My looks will belie that, Aunt Helen."

"It will seem so odd and peculiar. A girl always enjoys her second winter more than the first. Just when you have come to know everybody too! I hope you will reconsider this, dear. You had better order the dresses at any rate," she continued; "you might want to go when the time comes, and then it would be too late."

I shook my head decisively: "I am sorry to disappoint you, but my mind is made up."

Aunt Helen coughed again. "You are not disappointing *me;* it is only on your own account that I feel badly. You will make a great mistake, Virginia. Of course, dear, you have passed through a very unpleasant experience, which I am all the more able to appreciate from having had, as you are aware, sorrows of a similar kind. But painful as such experiences are for those called upon to undergo them, they are, I regret to say, far from uncommon; and if a young person who has suffered a disappointment were to turn his or her back on all entertainments, what, pray, would become of society?"

"Society will get along very well without me," I answered.

Aunt Helen knitted rapidly in silence, and the color mounted to her cheeks.

"You will make a great mistake, Virginia," she repeated, — "a great mistake. No young lady of your age can afford to make herself conspicuous by acting differently from other people. Do you wish to be called eccentric and peculiar?"

"I don't much care," said I with a spice of wickedness. "It might be rather attractive, I should think, to be different from everybody else."

"I can imagine who has been putting such ideas into your head. In my opinion one strong-minded woman in the family is quite enough," she said with a toss of her head.

I knew that she referred to Aunt Agnes, who had returned from Europe a few weeks before; therefore I said, —

"I have not exchanged a word with anybody on the subject."

"What *is* the reason, then, that you persist in being so contrary?" she exclaimed in a thoroughly worried tone, laying down her work on her lap.

"Because I have awakened to the fact that the little circle in which we move does not constitute the world," I answered, rather nettled by her solicitude. "I live as completely hedged about by conventions as the sleeping Beauty by the growth of a hundred years."

She opened her eyes in amazement. "All

women in every circle except the very lowest are hedged about by conventions," she replied severely. "What is it you wish to do?"

"I don't know that I wish to do anything. I am waiting for something to suggest itself."

"Does your father know of this?" she asked.

"Of what?"

"Of your intention to give up society."

"I have not thought it important enough to mention it to him."

"Important enough? I shall feel it my duty to inform him. We shall hear next that you have gone on the stage, or done something equally extraordinary."

"What do you mean?" I inquired with a wondering laugh.

"I have merely taken you at your own words. You have expressed dissatisfaction with the circle in which you live, and wish to try another. The only place where people are thoroughly unconventional is on the stage."

It was useless to discuss the matter further. Aunt Helen was not to be brought to look at it from my point of view, and I was resolute in my determination. I wished to meet and know a different set of people from those of the fashionable world. My ideas on the subject were vague. I had spoken the truth in saying that I was waiting for something to suggest itself.

There were of course plenty of earnest and interesting people, if one knew how to discover them. Naturally I often thought of Aunt Agnes, but pride interdicted me from applying to her. I felt that she had, to quote her own words, once for all made overtures to me, which I had declined, and that I could not bear the humiliation of going to her and confessing my ingratitude. When she came to spend the evening with us just after her return from Europe, her first remark to me had been: "Well, a pretty mess you and your Aunt Helen have made of it!" Beyond this she made no allusion to what had occurred, but she answered all my questions regarding her travels with the curtness of one who mistrusts the interest of the questioner.

However, as we had not met since, I felt in duty bound to pay my respects to her, and accordingly dropped in one day about luncheon time. She was not alone; and her visitor, who was a young woman some five years my senior, stopped short in her animated conversation as I entered, and swept down upon me with a wealth of facial expression in response to my Aunt's guttural —

"My niece!"

"This is too pleasant, Miss Harlan. I have heard about you so often, and wished to meet you. Now that we are acquainted, I do hope we shall be friends."

"This is Miss Kingsley, Virginia. You will not do amiss to follow in her footsteps," said Aunt Agnes, by way of setting me down where she considered I belonged, for I had not so far mortified the flesh as to alter my street costumes. As a consequence I was the pink of neatness in a new bonnet which contrasted itself already in my mind with the over-trimmed attire of my aunt's guest. I noticed that Miss Kingsley looked me over from head to foot with a sweeping glance as she spoke.

But I felt humble-minded, and disposed to seize any straw that might help me to realize my desire for new acquaintances. So I smiled sweetly, as though undisturbed by my aunt's severity, and greeted Miss Kingsley with more effusion than it was my wont to display toward strangers.

"I have heard that Miss Virginia Harlan is very clever," she said, opening and shutting her eyes in rapid succession, which I soon found was usual with her when she wished to be gracious, and which had much the effect of heat lightning on the beholder. "Weren't you at Tinker's Reach last summer?" she continued.

"She was," answered Aunt Agnes in a stern tone.

"Then you will be able to tell me if it is Mr. Dobbs or Dobson of Philadelphia, who is engaged to our Miss Bentley. I wrote it Dobbs, as seeming rather more distinguished. I agree with Mr. Spence that monosyllables are the most sympathetic."

"I am very sorry to say his name is Dobson," I answered.

Miss Kingsley sighed. "What a pity! Mere accuracy and art come so often into collision that it is difficult at times for us artists to do justice to both. I expended much thought on that item."

I felt greatly puzzled. It was evident she took it for granted that I knew who she was. But Aunt Agnes in attempting to enlighten me made my confusion all the greater.

"I presume, Virginia, that you are aware that Miss Kingsley is 'Alpha'?"

"'Alpha'?" I faltered.

"You must certainly have often read her column in the 'Sunday Mercury'?"

I looked embarrassed, for I never had. But the source of the item which had appeared about me in that newspaper was now apparent.

Miss Kingsley blushed, and giggled convulsively. "No offence. Quite natural, I'm sure. You have much better things to do than to read my articles, Miss Virginia. I only thought you might have happened to read Mr. Spence's 'Sonnet to Alpha' in our last issue."

I was obliged to admit that I had not; and feeling that it was as well to make a clean breast of my ignorance, I acknowledged that I had never heard of Mr. Spence.

Miss Kingsley gave a little gasp, and looked amused.

"Virginia! I am astonished," exclaimed Aunt Agnes. "Your father gave me to understand that you had been spending a portion of the summer in self-improvement. Mr. Spence is one of the most original thinkers in the community. I cannot believe it possible that you have never heard of him."

"Perhaps Miss Virginia may have read some of his poems or philosophy without knowing the author," suggested Miss Kingsley. "You must surely have heard of his 'Essay on the Economy of Speech,' which in my opinion is the most sympathetic thing he has done."

"One of the most valuable contributions to the literature of pure thought that we have had in many years," said Aunt Agnes.

I shook my head.

"Permit me," said Miss Kingsley, fumbling in a little reticule on her lap and taking therefrom one of several cards, which she handed to me.

"This is a schedule of his new course of lectures on Moderation. He regards moderation as the most valuable virtue of our civilization, and is devoting his life to the promulgation of its importance."

The printed card read as follows: —

LECTURES.

HAWTHORNE ROOMS.

SIX SUCCESSIVE SATURDAYS,

BEGINNING DECEMBER THE TWENTY-EIGHTH.

BY CHARLES LIVERSAGE SPENCE.

MODERATION.

December 28. General View of the Subject.
January   4. Tension and Torpor of the Nerves.
    „   11. The Economy of Speech.
    „   18. The Use and Abuse of Raiment.
    „   25. Overeating and Undereating.
February   1. Exuberance and Poverty in the Soul.

"They must be very interesting," said I. It was something at any rate to get a peep into the charmèd circle, even if I were too illiterate to share its membership; and I was eager to know more of the poet-philosopher, as I rightly judged him to be from Miss Kingsley's words.

"They are eminently suggestive," said she.

"You know him well I suppose."

"Mr. Spence? Yes. If I may say so," she simpered, with a rapid movement of her eyes, "your aunt and I were among the first to find him out."

"Is he young?"

"Just thirty. He celebrated his birthday only a fortnight ago. It was on that occasion that his 'Sonnet to Alpha' first saw the light."

"Is he good-looking?" I inquired somewhat ill advisedly, for Aunt Agnes made a gesture of impatience.

"His face is intellectual rather than handsome," answered Miss Kingsley. "Its expression is very striking and versatile. Fine, piercing eyes and waving hair, which he wears long. An intense individuality. But I should scarcely call him beautiful; interesting and highly sympathetic in appearance seems to me a more accurate description."

"If you mean by 'good-looking' to inquire if he is a fop, Virginia, you had better be undeceived on that score at once," said Aunt Agnes, with a toss of her head. "I don't suppose Mr. Spence has ever danced the German in his life."

"He is very particular about late hours," said Miss Kingsley; "that is a part of his system. He believes in moderation in all things, sleep as well as the contrary. He almost invariably retires before eleven, but he rises after eight hours of rest. He considers either more or less as deleterious to health. I am inclined to think though, if Miss Harlan will excuse my correcting her," she continued turning to Aunt Agnes, "that he has once or twice in his life danced the German; for he has told me that in order to develop his theory intelligently he has been obliged to study extremes. The happy mean cannot of course be estimated so intelligently by one who is without personal experience of the overmuch or undermuch he reprobates. Those are his own phrases for expressing excess or undue limitation, and to me they seem exquisite specimens of nomenclature. But as I was saying, Mr. Spence has in the course of his investigations sampled, if I may so speak, almost every sensation or series of sensations to which human nature is susceptible. For instance, he once spent the night in a tomb, so as to experience what he has so exquisitely styled in a poem on the subject 'the extremity of doleful comprehension.' You were alluding to the lines only yesterday, Miss Harlan."

"They are Miltonic in their grim power," said Aunt Agnes.

" Then again, he lived upon dog and horse during the time of the Commune at Paris. He says it was worth the experience of an ordinary lifetime as illustrating the crucial test of discomfort. So in like manner he has experienced the extremes of luxury and pleasure. I have been given to understand that he even felt it his duty to intoxicate himself upon one occasion, in order to be able to demolish more conclusively the arguments of either form of intemperance; for he considers total abstinence as almost, if not quite, on a level with over indulgence. One's instinct of course shrinks at first from the idea of a deliberate clouding of the senses being ever pardonable, but the more one examines the matter the more innocent does it appear; and I freely admit that I have come to regard an offence against morals committed in the interest of science as not only excusable, but in some cases a positive duty."

"But," said Aunt Agnes, taking up the thread of her previous remark for my further edification, "however Mr. Spence may have conducted himself in the past for the sake of discipline, his habits to-day are essentially sober and serious."

"Oh, dear, yes!" exclaimed Miss Kingsley; "he is intensely in earnest, and discountenances all mere vanities of life. And yet, withal, it is his aim to pursue the happy mean. He believes in rational amusements, and is very sympathetic in congenial society. If you have no pleasanter engagement for next Wednesday evening, Miss Virginia, I shall be charmed to have you take tea with me at my rooms in the Studio Building. I expect Mr. Spence and one or two other friends to be present."

"With great pleasure," I answered; and I felt quite elated by the invitation. My ambition to form new associations was about to be realized apparently.

"I have hopes that Mr. Spence will consent to illustrate his theory of the Economy of Speech on that evening," continued Miss Kingsley. "As yet the science is in embryo, and naturally but a very small number of people are sufficiently familiar with the practical details of the theory to make it advisable to adopt it in general conversation. But with sympathetic friends he may feel disposed to make the experiment."

"You are extremely fortunate, Virginia," said Aunt Agnes, with emphasis.

"I should try in vain to be worthy of such an opportunity; but I am very much obliged to you, Miss Kingsley," I answered humbly.

"You will soon learn," she said, rising to go. "I am so glad to have had the pleasure of meeting you at last. I have alluded to you in my column on one or two occasions, but this is the first time I have had the gratification of seeing you in person. Perhaps you can tell me," she continued, still holding my hand, "whether there is any truth in the reported engagement of our Miss Leonard to Mr. Clarence Butterfield. And if you happen to know who are to be the bridesmaids at the wedding of Miss Newton, of Philadelphia, to our Mr. Lester, I shall consider it very friendly of you to tell me."

This made me feel very uncomfortable, for I could not decide on the spur of the moment whether it would be more charitable to my friends to tell the truth, or to remain silent and let their affairs be garbled.

"I want to put in something," she urged, noticing my hesitation. "I shall either contradict or confirm the report of the engagement in our next issue. Of course, artistically it makes little difference to me which; but it is much more satisfactory to the immediate friends to have an item correct, — just as the friends of a person who sits for a portrait prefer to have the likeness speaking, whereas to the painter it is much more important whether the *tout ensemble* is a work of art. To obtain a portrait one can always have recourse to the photographer; and so to insure mere accuracy in a social jotting, it is easy to pay for it as an advertisement. But artists stand upon a different footing. Am I clear? And I trust that you agree with me. It will do just as well on Wednesday; and if you should hear any other items of interest in my line, please note them. You have no idea of the competition I have to encounter. Some artists go so far as to invent their material, but it is not considered strictly professional. Well, I must run along. Don't forget, Wednesday at eight," and Miss Kingsley whisked out of the room, leaving me in a dazed condition.

The collection of social gossip was apparently her regular business, which she not only was ready to acknowledge, but gloried in,—just as a merchant might take pride in his bargains, or a lawyer in his arguments. There was a certain savor of self-reliance and proprietorship in her use of the word " our," by which it was evident to me, though I was sadly puzzled at first, that she distinguished Bostonians from those who lived elsewhere. But horrified as I was by the general idea of such a calling, I could not help feeling amused, and even rather admired Miss Kingsley's independence and enterprising spirit. She was a shade vulgar to be sure, but in my present frame of mind I was disposed to rank intellectual superiority above mere refinement of manner. I believed that Miss Kingsley, although but a few years older than myself, could put me to the blush in the matter of literary attainments and general information.

Aunt Agnes was plainly of that opinion, for she aroused me from my reflections by the remark,—

" A rare opportunity is afforded you, Virginia, for mental discipline. I can see that Miss Kingsley has taken a fancy to you. She is not a person who goes off at a tangent. She must have discerned capabilities for culture in you, or she would never have invited you to one of her entertainments. To you, who are accustomed to society fine speeches that mean nothing, it will probably occur that she is asking you on my account. Nothing of the sort. There is not an ounce of affectation in her. She has asked you because she wants you; and I can only add that if you neglect after this to seek improvement, you will be guilty of a deliberate sacrifice of talents for which there can be no excuse. Yes, talents. There is no use in mincing matters; you have talents. I have always thought so, which is the reason why I have taken so much trouble to keep you from evil courses. Your father has given me to understand that you have begun to listen to the voice of experience. I tried to save you from experience by counsel, but you scoffed at my words. You have providentially had your eyes opened before it was too late. You have suffered, and I do not wish to add to your mortification by reproach. Let by-gones be by-gones, and I trust to hear no more of Mr. Gale and his associates."

"Dale, Aunt Agnes," I said firmly.

She shrugged her shoulders impatiently. "What difference does it make whether it is Dale or Gale? You heard what Miss Kingsley said just now about the unimportance of accuracy in trivial matters. You knew perfectly well whom I meant. Let me caution you again, Virginia, against an undue estimate of ceremony and form. It is the spirit that is of value, not the mere letter. Especially should you bear this in mind in the society of such people as you will meet on Wednesday evening. The world is a large place, and only in the circle in which you have been brought up is excessive regard paid to insignificant details. Sensible people have other things to think about."

"Does Mr. Spence belong to Boston?" I asked, anxious to find out all I could about the celebrity.

But this remark was not more happy than the last. Aunt Agnes pursed up her lips and said, —

"If you mean, was he born in Beacon Street, no, he was not. Dreadful as it may seem to you, I know nothing of either his father or his mother. But you will learn when you are a little wiser, that genius in order to be recognized and admired is not obliged to produce parents."

"You misunderstood me, Aunt Agnes. I merely wished to know if he were a foreigner or not."

"He has lived everywhere I believe, and is cosmopolitan, as all great men are. He is one of the few characters really worth knowing in our community. His philosophic and hygienic thoughts surpass his poetry in worth, in the opinion of the best judges."

"And Miss Kingsley,—does she write at all?"

"Certainly. Did she not tell you that she is the compiler of the weekly column of fashionable items in the 'Sunday Mercury'?"

"Yes," said I, "but that is scarcely literature."

Aunt Agnes did not answer for a moment. "You have judged hastily, and consequently have misjudged. If you were to ask me whether I think Miss Kingsley's present occupation is proportionate to her abilities, I should answer 'no.' She would herself admit that it was hack-work,—though, mind you, even hack-work can be redeemed by an artistic spirit, as she has so adequately explained to you. All young women have not independent fortunes, and such as are without means are obliged to take whatever they can find to do in the line of their professions. I agree with your implication that society items do not constitute literature, but they are stepping stones to higher things. Which is the more creditable, pray, to collect and chronicle the social customs of the age in which you live, foolish as they may be, or to be one of the giddy and frivolous creatures whose doings are thus compiled as a warning to posterity, or to excite its jeers? The one is work, earnest though humble; the other, a sheer dissipation of the energies of life."

I felt that this was aimed at me; but as I made no response, Aunt Agnes continued: —

"Do not mistake my meaning now, and say that I wish you to become a collector of fashionable information. On the contrary, I should much regret to see you anything of the kind. By the very circumstance that Providence has given you the means to pick and choose, you are marked out for work of a less superficial order. But you must not under-value others who are less able to consult their own preferences. Miss Kingsley is a young woman of decided capabilities for original composition. Mr. Spence has spoken to me of her in terms of the highest praise. Because she is obliged for her support to cater to the popular taste for social intelligence, it by no means follows that she does not employ her spare hours to better advantage. I shall not violate any confidences I may have received, in saying that Miss

Kingsley is capable of literary production of a high order."

"But," said I after a moment's silence, "you cannot approve of the custom of putting the private affairs of people into print, Aunt Agnes?"

"It is preferable at least to wasting the best years of one's life in fashionable folly," she replied with some asperity.

As I saw it would be hopeless to pursue the conversation on this head without danger of further disagreement, I rose to take my leave. But when I stooped to kiss her, she took me by the hand and said with much seriousness, but with a purpose to be kindly, —

"I have much greater hopes, Virginia, I frankly confess, regarding the stability of your character than when I last conversed with you. You may depend on whatever assistance lies in my power; but let me impress upon you that the cultivation which your talents befit you to attain, cannot be reached without strenuous exertions on your own part."

"I shall do all I can to make the most of my advantages, Aunt Agnes, you may depend upon it; and I thank you heartily for your offer of help. I hope I have done with frivolity forever."

"My niece marry a whipper-snapper like that Mr. Gale, indeed! Tell me!"

I had not the hardihood to correct her again, and so we parted.

II.

WEDNESDAY was only the day after to-morrow, but in the interim I bought a copy of Mr. Spence's Poems and also his volume of Essays, which contained "The Economy of Speech," "The Overmuch and the Undermuch," and "The Equipoise of Passion," the last-named being an exposition of the selfishness of unlimited love. His poems, which were for the most part written in early youth, were in striking contrast to the essays in tone. Indeed, in the extracts from the newspaper criticisms prefixed to the volume of verse he was in several instances spoken of as the Baudelaire of America. They were alternately morbid and convivial in style, and were concerned largely with death, the rapture of the wine-cup, or the bitterness of unreciprocated attachment. I was inclined to be shocked at the outset, for I had never read anything of the sort before, as Baudelaire was then merely a name to me. I even took the book to my own room from an unwillingness to leave it lying on the parlor table. But after the first surprise and qualms I found myself rather fascinated by the unusual nature of the man. At one moment he appeared to be flushed with ecstasy, and the next in the depths, — an alternative so opposed to the tenor of his later philosophy that I was fairly puzzled, until I reflected that these poems had undoubtedly been composed during his novitiate, while he was testing the extremes of life. It was obvious, if his verse was any criterion, that he had been very thorough in his investigations, and that Miss Kingsley's estimate of his offences against morality was not an over-statement, to say the least. But my curiosity was aroused to meet a person whose ideas and experiences were so signally unlike my own, especially in view of the seeming total transition of his sentiments as portrayed in his subsequent prose writings. I thought them a little vague, but extremely interesting. The skeleton of his system was unfolded in the essay on the "Overmuch and the Undermuch." Therein he sought to show in a general way the advantages of moderation. Nothing overmuch was the key-note of his theory, — an aphorism which found an analogy in the old Greek motto οὐδὲν ἄγαν, which he adduced to prove the antiquity of the virtue, little as it had been practised. He represented moderation as the great principle upon which the future progress of civilization depended. Without heed to the restrictions which it imposed, human nature must despair of perfection. He ventured to predict that rigorous self-restraint, continued through successive generations, would appreciably lengthen the average duration of life, and although without more sufficient data it would be incautious to make extravagant claims, it seemed to him by no means improbable that death might in the end be conquered, or at least indefinitely postponed. The science was as yet embryonic, and until the general interest of the world in its development had been awakened, investigation in order to be trustworthy must needs be slow.

Treating the subject in detail, he applied his theory to various departments of life. His own investigations he alleged to be still very incomplete, and in this first volume he had only touched upon two subdivisions, — conversation and love, the presentation of his ideas regarding which were contained in the essays already spoken of, " The Economy of Speech," and " The Equipoise of Passion." In the first named of these he laid down as a broad general statement that some people talk too much and others too little. Here, as in other functions, either extreme was disastrous. Prolixity of speech produced avoidance of the offender, and silence tended to syncope of the language. The causes of either fault were in his opinion far to seek, and lay less in the nature of the individual than in the essence of orthography and diction. Tautology was the blemish of written and vocal speech. Too many symbols were used to express an idea, and nothing was left to the imagination of the reader or hearer. Redundancy of expression was the *vade mecum* of the bore, and on the other hand there was no reason to believe that the sound of their own words was the cause why many people were so silent. It was common to hear that a man was afraid to hear himself talk. By reducing therefore the signs of speech, a stimulus would be given to the reserved and a curb imposed upon the verbose.

The primary principle employed to effect this was ellipsis, but an accurate understanding of the intelligence of the hearer was requisite in order to become proficient. The alphabet was not disturbed or abbreviated. The radical change was in the dismemberment of sentences.

And here it was obvious that a greater number of words could be omitted without destroying the sense with a clever listener than with a dull person. His statistics showed that two individuals thoroughly conversant with the system could discourse rationally upon intricate topics by the use of single words and even single monosyllables in place of entire sentences; and this led him to believe that as the race grew in intelligence, speech would finally become a rudimentary organ and cease to be. Nor was this inconsistent with his general theory; for in his opinion the gradual tendency of all mere physical attributes was to coalesce with mind. In an analogous way the time would come when mankind instead of eating too much or too little would not eat at all. But the first stage in this gradual evolution must be a repression of extremes resulting in moderation. It was to effect a recognition of this that his labors were directed.

I expected to be even more interested in the essay on "The Equipoise of Passion," remembering the intense character of his amatory verse. But the philosophical terms were so numerous that I found myself at a loss as to his meaning at times. His treatment of the subject was quite different; for whereas (he explained) speech was a physical attribute and destined to give place to some other method of affinity, love was psychical in its essence, and hence immortal. But he maintained that moderation should control spirit no less than matter, and that either undue exaltation or a lack of sentiment were inconsistent with the noblest type of altruism.

Love in order to be perfect must be rational and cognizant, as he expressed it. The beloved object should be enthroned, but without exaggeration, and yet with ecstasy. The defect of love as it at present existed was that it was either an hallucination or a bargain. This should not be; but on the other hand the equipoise of passion like the equipoise of religion, — of which it was in his opinion the peer, and with which it was in a certain sense blended, — was attainable only by exceptional souls. The equipoise of speech or of raiment or of appetite was within the grasp of an average human being, but only a few spirits in a generation enjoyed the perfection of love. This was the crown of his philosophy; but it was here that he felt the need of further investigation before endeavoring to demonstrate the remedy by means of which this number might be increased, so as finally to include all earnest souls. An immature statement would impair the authority of the more elemental truth he had sought to establish; but he hoped in a subsequent volume to complete the exposition of this last step in his system.

III.

I RAPPED at Miss Kingsley's door on Wednesday evening with some trepidation, but with a sense of pleasurable excitement. I felt that her entertainment was sure to be very unlike those to which I was accustomed. In the first place, the idea of combining home and business quarters in one apartment was new to me, and seemed slightly incongruous. The Studio Building was large, and she had doubtless a host of neighbors who lived in the same manner; but they were a class with whom I was wholly unacquainted. Miss Kingsley's rooms were in the top story where, as I reflected, she could enjoy fresh air and escape the everlasting tinkling of the horse-cars and rattle of vehicles in the street below.

She opened the door herself, and her face assumed its most radiant expression as she recognized me.

"This is too delightful, Miss Harlan!"

I found myself face to face with several people whom she hastened to introduce. The only familiar name was that of Mr. Paul Barr, which I instantly recollected to have seen on the dedicatory page of Mr. Spence's volume of poems. The inscription read, "To my soul's brother, Paul Barr," and hence I gazed at the stranger with interest.

From Mr. Barr I got the impression of a handsome but dishevelled looking man of large stature, with a coal-black beard and dark piercing eyes, which he bent upon me ardently as he bowed his figure in what might well be styled a profound and lavish obeisance. He wore a velveteen coat and a large cherry neck-tie, the flowing ends of which added to his general air of disorder. The other names — to which I gave slight heed, for their owners were not especially significant in appearance — were Mr. Fleisch, a short, small German with eye-glasses, and Mrs. Marsh, a fat, genial matron of five-and-forty.

All this I took in at a glance, for Miss Kingsley conducted me immediately into her boudoir (as she called it), to lay aside my wraps.

"Has he not soulful eyes?" she asked.

"Who?" said I, though I knew to whom she must refer.

"Mr. Barr."

"What is he?" said I.

"A Bohemian, dear," she replied in a tone of satisfaction.

" Really?"

I had long wished to meet a member of that mysterious brotherhood, of which of course I had heard and read.

" Yes. He is a poet-painter, and a great friend of Mr. Spence. Have you never seen his pictures? Even Mr. Spence admits that they possess the *abandon* of genius, although he disapproves of *abandon*. Their views to-day are totally dissimilar, but yet their friendship is sympathetic as ever. Is it not inspiring?"

"Mr. Spence is coming, I hope?"

"Oh, yes. I expect him every moment, and I have made Mr. Barr promise to get him to give us an exposition. Not knowing how you might feel, Virginia (may I call you Virginia? It seems so much more natural after having heard your aunt always speak of you in that way. Thank you, dear. And if you will call me Lucretia, I shall feel much flattered), — not knowing how you might feel about coming where there was no matron, I asked Mrs. Marsh to join us. We do not regard it of importance, and you will not a little later; but just at first it is perhaps as well. Do you know Mr. Fleisch by reputation? He plays with an artistic charm, rare even in this musical epoch. He is a follower of Mr. Spence, and is seeking to apply his principles of moderation to music with striking success. Ah! you must excuse me, dear, it is his knock."

I understood that she referred to Mr. Spence, and I waited an instant to put a finishing touch to my toilet before following her into the other room. For I had still something of the old Adam, or rather of the old Eve, left in me; so that I must confess my eagerness for culture was not without a spice of coquetry, half unconscious though it were.

Mr. Spence from his appearance was fairly entitled to be called a moderationist. He had nothing of the splendid savagery of Mr. Paul Barr, whose luxuriant and matted head of hair now struck my attention, nor the student-like insignificance of Mr. Fleisch. He was neither tall nor short, stout nor inadequately spare; and he was in evening dress like anybody else. Had I met him without knowing who he was, I should never have imagined him a celebrity. This was my first impression, but a second look at his face revealed firm though thin lips, and small nervous eyes that were full of fire when in movement. It was not however until I heard him speak that I recovered from my disappointment. "Be it so," was all he said in reply to some remark addressed to him; but the enunciation of the words was so musical, so soft and winning, yet so clear and authoritative, that I was spell-bound for an instant and quite lost my composure as Miss Kingsley, becoming aware of my presence, proceeded to make us acquainted.

The backs of all the company except Mr. Spence had been turned to me, for Mr. Barr was fulfilling his promise of persuading his friend to introduce his system of speech as the order of the evening. The ecstatic expression of Miss Kingsley's face, as well as the few words I had heard him utter, were sufficient to show that he had been successful; but winking her eyes more rapidly than ever she whispered in my ear with an imitation as I thought of her master's style, —

"It is to be."

Almost immediately Mr. Spence, whose bow I had thought rather formal and like that of the rest of the world, came up to me and said: —

"Welcome, Miss Harlan, to our circle. I know your aunt, — a massive woman intellectually, and my benefactor. As I think our hostess has already intimated to you, it is the wish of some of the company that I should give a practical illustration of certain views regarding the essence of speech peculiar to me, of which it may be you have heard from your kinswoman or others, and which are a corollary of the general truth or virtue known to the outside world as moderation. I have, however, some delicacy in inflicting so great an incubus — for it must seem such to the uninitiated — upon one who like you is of the *beau monde* and used to its smooth ways. I speak knowingly, for I too in my day belonged to the *beau monde*, and am familiar with the easy, however volatile, flow of speech incident thereto."

"Do not mind me, I pray," said I. "Indeed, I have read your essays as well as your poems, Mr. Spence, and am very anxious to understand your system practically."

"Be it so," he replied. "I did not wish to inflict myself unduly. Art should be sensitive. Do you not agree with me, Miss Harlan?"

"How exquisite!" I heard Miss Kingsley whisper to Mr. Fleisch, with whom she was standing a few feet distant gazing at the master.

It was Mr. Paul Barr who answered the question for me: —

"No, Miss Harlan, Art should be aggressive; Art should be ardent. I do not agree with Mr. Spence. In fact, we never agree upon any subject. But we are friends, life-long, bosom friends. Shake, Charles, shake! we have not given the grip and pressure of amity to-night."

He spoke in a deep, sonorous base, and extended to his friend a hirsute hand.

"It is true we belong to different schools, Mr. Barr and I, Miss Harlan," said Mr. Spence. "He believes in the supremacy of the untrammelled, as his poems and pictures show; I, on the contrary, give my voice to equipoise. But, as he has well said, we are devoted friends."

"You shall judge between us," continued Paul Barr addressing me. "Which is better, the free undulation of self, or eternal tension?"

"A fine antithesis," murmured Miss Kingsley.

"*Mein Gott!* but it is not true, that free undulation of self. It deceives, it deludes: it is a — what word is it I am seeking? — a — eh — I have it, — boomerang, — a boomerang that plagues the inventor," said Mr. Fleisch.

"Refuted, well refuted!" said Mr. Spence. "Fleisch has hit the mark. The overmuch is indeed a boomerang. Thanks, Bernard, for the epigram," he added, turning to the little German.

Everybody clapped their hands except myself and Mr. Barr. I preferred to remain neutral. As for the artist, he stood stroking his beard fiercely with his eyes fixed on the ceiling.

At this moment the door opened, and a maid-servant announced tea.

Mr. Spence looked at Miss Kingsley interrogatively. "From this moment, please," said she.

He shrugged his shoulders and sighed; and as we walked in to tea together Miss Kingsley whispered that he was about to practise his theory.

"Of course, Virginia dear, every one will understand that you are a novice, and you will be at liberty to talk in your natural manner. The rest of us are expected to assist Mr. Spence as far as possible. I am all in a flutter; I know I shall break down."

The room in which we took tea was a veritable snuggery. The servant found it difficult to get round the table, and there was a strong smell of the frying-pan owing to the vicinity of the tiny kitchen. But these inconveniences, if they were so to be called, merely added to my zest and enjoyment. Here, indeed, was agreeable and talented society! Aunt Agnes was right,— my associates hitherto had been frivolous and volatile. The world of fashion was a sham. What a contrast,— I could not help making it,— between the insipid speeches of my former friends and the clever talk of this purely literary circle, where ideas and scholarship were recognized and crowned.

Mr. Spence and Mr Barr sat on either side of Miss Kingsley, and I glanced from the one to the other, debating with myself whether I preferred the bold strong beauty of the artist, or the subtile and more delicate traits of feature of the philosopher. For though I had begun by regarding Mr. Spence almost as commonplace in appearance, the earnestness of his manner and the serious fervor of his eyes gave him an expression of having a deep and genuine belief in his own theories, which when compared with the impetuous but more volatile air of Paul Barr commended him to my respect and admiration even while I was flattered by the gallantries of his rival.

It was Mr. Barr who first broke the silence after we sat down to table, by asking me if I had not passed the summer at Tinker's Reach. As he spoke in the ordinary guise, I was surprised until it occurred to me that as a member of another school he could hardly be expected, even from courtesy or friendship, to practise doctrines to which he could not subscribe.

"Yes," said I.

"Malaria," began Mr. Spence.

There was a little murmur of expectation, and Mr. Fleisch brimming over with excitement said, "Bad drainage."

"No excuse. Sea near. Inhabitants should agitate question," continued Mr. Spence.

"Everybody appearance of health notwithstanding," exclaimed Miss Kingsley.

"Overmuch ozone," said Mr. Spence.

"Unhealthy stimulus. Reaction later," added the little German.

"Are we clear? Air of Tinker's Reach you know; so clever," whispered Miss Kingsley leaning toward me behind Mr. Spence's chair. "Sure I shall break down."

I nodded to give her encouragement. All this was somewhat bewildering, but I was able to follow the conversation. I was conscious too of Mr. Barr's eyes fixed upon me with intensity. He would eat hurriedly for a moment, and then fold his arms and listen with his brow almost buried in his black bristly beard, and his glance centred on me.

The talk went on briskly. Mrs. Marsh presently joined in ; and after the discussion of the atmospheric conditions of Tinker's Reach was exhausted, a criticism of a recent volume of poetry followed, in which Mr. Fleisch and Mrs. Marsh took sides against the other two. At times I lost the thread of the argument, but for the most part I understood them perfectly. Mr. Spence was by far the most proficient. It was wonderful how he was able to express frequently in a single word the idea of an entire sentence. I listened with eager and increasing interest. Every now and then Mr. Barr interrupted the conversation with a torrent of words, sometimes by way of soliloquizing comment on the views expressed, and occasionally addressed to me. In the latter case I always put my fingers on my lips and smiled, a course which had the effect of silencing him for the time being. Meanwhile everybody eat with appetite of the good things provided; and the artist-poet, as though to show his contempt for the doctrines of moderation, helped himself again and again from a crystal pitcher of claret-cup that was at his elbow.

Of a sudden, to my great consternation, Mr. Spence looked directly at me and said,—

"Paris?"

All my ideas seemed to desert me on the spot. But by a rapid inspiration I shook my head and said,—

"Never."

"There during Commune," continued my interrogator, and I saw from Miss Kingsley's radiant and encouraging smile and nod that I had been right in my assumption that he wished to know if I had ever been there.

"Really!" I said, emboldened.

"Grisly," said he.

"Cat!" almost hissed Mr. Fleisch in his excitement.

"Dog!" said Mrs. Marsh.

"Horse!" exclaimed Miss Kingsley.

Fortunately I recalled what Miss Kingsley had told me regarding Mr. Spence's early experiences in search of extremes, so that I was not as nonplussed as might perhaps have been expected by these ejaculations.

"Gruesome!" I said, with a determination to acquit myself creditably.

"Unsympathetic!" added Miss Kingsley, rather unnecessarily as I thought.

"Not so bad. Lived on them for days," said Mr. Spence, still addressing me. "Time of my novitiate."

"Where self undulates freely there is no novitiate, for all is allowable," exclaimed Paul Barr fiercely; and he filled another goblet. I almost felt afraid of his gaze, it had become so intense and ardent. I tried not to look in his direction, though there was an originality and fascination about him that made it next to impossible not to steal an occasional glance across the table.

Mr. Spence held up his hand deprecatingly in answer to his friend's tirade, while little Fleisch like a trusty retainer exclaimed once more with fierceness, —

"Boomerang!"

Mr. Spence again turned to me, "Worse; night in tomb!"

"Beside corpse!" explained Mr. Fleisch.

The ladies shivered.

"Trifle," murmured Mr. Spence.

"Extremity of doleful comprehension!" said Miss Kingsley.

I felt that my opportunity had come. Carried away as I was by the interest and excitement of the proceedings, I repeated from memory, without embarrassment, the first five lines of Mr. Spence's poem entitled "A Fragment (written after a night passed in the grave)."

" I lay a living soul within the tomb, —
A ghastly cabin damp with church-yard loam,
Where worms are rampant and where night enthrones
Darkness and horror, dust, decay, and bones;
Extremity of doleful comprehension."

There was a murmur of applause.

" Exquisitely apposite!" cried Mr. Fleisch, and for the first time he surveyed me through his eye-glass with evident interest.

Mr. Spence bent forward in acknowledgement of the quotation. Mrs. Marsh repeated after her neighbor, —

" Exquisitely apposite!"

"A fine passage and finely rendered," said Paul Barr; and he sighed (though it was not obvious why), and emptied his glass.

I glanced at my hostess. To my surprise she was examining a tea-cup, and as she looked up I saw that her face was no longer radiant. Our eyes met, and in an instant the truth flashed upon me. She was jealous! Without design I had too much absorbed the attention of the lion of the evening. Or was it Paul Barr's glances that I had estranged?

For a moment I was both confounded and regretful, but in the next I had decided that her resentment, if it were real, was unjustifiable. Any success I had won was unpremeditated, and there was no reason why I should be otherwise than natural, or decline to use to the best advantage the talents which Heaven had given me. It was Mr. Spence undoubtedly whom my hostess considered her especial property. She would have earlier indicated her disapproval had the artist-poet been the offender, for his glances had been unmistakable in their direction from the first. I felt in no wise to blame. It was not my intention or ambition to captivate either of these literary gentry; but if in my endeavors to appreciate and sympathize with their thoughts and theories I had been able to win their regard, was it for me to heed the envy of one who grudged me this trifling tribute to my enthusiasm? Assuredly not. Therefore I resolved to act exactly as if I were unconscious of Miss Kingsley's disapprobation.

I was aroused from these reflections by hearing Mr. Fleisch call me by name. He informed me in the curtailed speech we were using that he had set to music the words of the poem from which I had quoted, and that after tea he would, with the permission of the company, play it to us. From him and Mr. Spence conjointly I then learned that he had followed out the principles of moderation in a number of original productions. Most musical scores were too long, he said, — just as many people talked too much, — and he was seeking to popularize even classical works by abbreviating them, after the fashion adopted by Mr. Spence in regard to conversation. In this manner formidable pieces, like oratorios and symphonies, could be made congenial and instructive to those who usually found them tedious. In music as in literature the idea was the main consideration, and in Mr. Fleisch's opinion the vehicle by which it was conveyed should be as little cumbersome as possible. Acting on this principle, he had in one instance reduced an entire symphony to eight chords without destroying the charm. In music compression was possible to a greater extent, he believed, than in any other art.

While Mr. Fleisch and Mr. Spence were devoting their attention to making this new offshoot of the system clear to me, I was occasionally distracted by the behavior of Miss Kingsley, who was audibly using my name in the course of a whispered colloquy with Mr. Barr. The artist's eyes still never strayed from my face, but his ear was open to his neighbor's confidences; and I could gather — for it is difficult to avoid listening where one is the subject of conversation — that she was representing me as belonging to the world of fashion, and present merely upon sufferance. I noticed too that, curiously enough, Mr. Spence seemed attracted by the sound of my name, and would now and then secretly lend an ear to what was being said upon his other side. In fact I soon made up my mind that it was for his benefit Miss Kingsley was talking. She hoped to undermine my influence by an unflattering description of my doings in society. It was doubtless her cue to make her guests regard me as a frivolous character.

Naturally I was indignant, and my pride was aroused. To be sure I was in her debt for the opportunity she had given me of meeting these literary friends, but that gave her no license to misrepresent me, in a light which in my present humor was the most distasteful she could have selected. Under the spur of pique I redoubled my graciousness toward Mr. Spence and Mr. Fleisch, and likewise watched my opportunity to court the artist with a smile, whereupon he sighed again and reached out his hand for the crystal pitcher; but it was empty.

Miss Kingsley, however, was not one to quit the field without a struggle. So successful were my efforts that she was forced to sit silent and with a smile on her lip, from her obligations as a hostess; but I knew she was preparing a revenge.

It came sooner than I expected. Taking advantage of a pause in the conversation, caused by Mr. Spence leaning forward to explain to me on paper the rudiments of an attempt he had been making to apply the principles of the Economy of Speech to arithmetical problems, she whispered in an aside to Paul Barr, but so loud as to be audible to every one at table, —

"Three millions at least."

Impertinent as this reference to my worldly prospects was, I should not have regarded it as of importance but for the strange behavior of Mr. Spence, whose hand at the announcement shook in writing like an aspen leaf. He looked up at me with an expression of mingled pain and inquiry, which was so completely earnest that my own eyes drooped on meeting his. An embarrassing silence ensued for an instant, and then with a bound Paul Barr rose from his chair, and flinging himself down before the piano began to dash off a wild, exuberant production that suggested the lawless but triumphant pæan of some heathen divinity.

As we returned to the other room I felt instinctively that my prestige with Mr. Spence had been impaired by the whisper of Miss Kingsley. His attentions ceased, and as a consequence Mr. Fleisch also neglected me. I took a seat on the sofa by the side of Mrs. Marsh. In an opposite corner my rival and the two moderationists were examining a manuscript without apparent consciousness of my existence. The sudden transposition of affairs made me sensitive. Paul Barr still sat at the piano executing his delirious fantasy, and ever and anon looking back over his shoulder at me. He at least was faithful. But it was not admiration I sought. I wished for respect for my intelligence, and to be considered a promising proselyte of culture. I seemed a few moments ago to have won this recognition from the entire company, and now I was an outcast.

As fortune would have it, the mystery was explained a few minutes later through the efficacy of Mrs. Marsh. We entered into conversation, and almost immediately she volunteered certain details regarding Miss Kingsley, brought about primarily by my inquiring her age.

"How old? Lucretia Kingsley will never see thirty again, no matter how hard she tries to look younger. She's a fine-appearing girl though, and a stylish dresser. She makes a pretty penny, I understand, out of the work she does for the newspapers. Folks say," — here she lowered her voice; and let it be added at the same time that I felt some compunctions at her not continuing to use the economic system, but in my interest to learn her secret I was weak enough to let her go on, — " folks say that she and Mr. Spence will hit it off together some day. I guess she's thrifty, too, when she's not at her books. Did you notice how worked up he was when your three millions were spoken of? I could see he'd taken a fancy to you, but when that came out he had to drop you like a hot cake."

"What do you mean?" I asked, too much astonished to be upset by her colloquial style.

"It's the only part of his philosophy that I don't altogether take to, for it doesn't seem quite natural to me to turn one's back on what Heaven sends in the way of income. I'm an out-and-out convert to his doctrines into the bargain. I used to believe in having a good time, and all that sort of nonsense; but I've come to see that what he calls equipoise is the true road to happiness, and that it's best to leave off a bit hungry if you want to live to a green old age. I suppose you've heard his lecture on 'Overeating and Undereating'? If you have n't, don't fail to go the next time he delivers it. There's more good sound medicine in two sentences of that than in all the apothecary shops in creation. I went to hear him by accident too, for I'm not partial to lectures as a rule. I had the dyspepsia bad, and had spent more money on physic and the doctors than it would take to support Mr. Spence for the rest of his born days. They all wanted one of two things, — either that I should stuff myself or starve myself. One was for having me eat every five minutes, and the next made me weigh everything that went into my stomach. But Mr. Spence took the bull by the horns when he said, 'Some people eat too much, and some eat too little. Preserve a happy medium!' And that's what I've been doing ever since, and the consequence is I could eat nails if I was pressed hard."

"But eating is quite a different thing from income," she continued, relieving at last my impatience; "and I can't see the sense of his idea that people should n't keep more than just enough money to live on. It's a part of his system, as he calls it, I know; and if he says that human nature would be better with less, I am not the one to gainsay him, for there's no young man of his years in the city smarter than Mr. Spence, and he may be right. I can say, though, that before this it has stood in the way of his marrying. Only two years ago there was a young lady from New York just crazy to get him. She was real elegant too, and folks say he fancied her. But she was very rich, just as you are; and she was n't willing — and I don't blame her either — to give up every blessed cent because he wanted her to. But he is bent on carrying his principles of moderation into daily practice, and there's no use in resisting him. It's rare he takes a liking so strong as he took to you to-night, and perhaps it was best for both of you that the truth came out when it did."

"Very much," I answered in a dazed tone.

Mrs. Marsh's confidences had mystified me more than ever. Of course I could no longer doubt Miss Kingsley's jealousy; but it was not equally apparent to me why Mr. Spence should have felt obliged to change his behavior so precipitately because of my wealth. Surely he could tolerate even if he did not advocate the possession of riches. I was young, and had much to learn. It was possible that when I came to hear his arguments, I might be convinced and ready to sacrifice my prospects of a large income to the demands of a noble philosophy. If it were a question of marriage, I could readily understand his insisting that his bride should comply with his views in this respect. But I was merely a guest of Miss Kingsley, an acquaintance whom he might never see again. His conduct seemed to me irrational and strange. I could not believe that he had cast me off because of an unwillingness to offend his hostess, for he had appeared wholly absorbed in my presence until her impertinent speech in regard to my property had put an abrupt end to his complaisance.

Meanwhile Mr. Barr had finished his pæan and seated himself near me. There was no mistaking the glances he cast, and out of respect to myself I chose to exhibit some coldness of manner in response to his remarks, which were an ardent defence of passion and what he called *verve* in music, literature, and art. Keen enjoyment, he said, was never to be found in restraint; and if extremes tended to shorten human life, a short existence crowned with pleasure was preferable to four-score and ten years of dull uniformity. The giant trees of the forest, the reddest roses of the garden, and the fairest faces in Christendom must be frowned on as noxious if the doctrine of moderation was to prevail. For were not they extremes? Yet rob the world of them, and where would a recompense be found for their loss? In ordinary growths, in the every-day rose, in commonplace beauty? Heaven forbid! and he pulled at his beard, and his fine eyes flashed in the fulness of his excitement.

Mrs. Marsh looked shocked, and took up the cudgels against him in defence of the opposite principles, so that I was able to keep silent and wonder. He would fain deify passion, he said; and there were two passions which no human agency could stem or curb,—the passion for wealth, and the passion of love. Thereat he looked at me again, with so much eloquence of expression that I had to blush and turn my head away.

Then the little German, Mr. Fleisch, sat down at the piano and performed a series of pieces in illustration of what he had explained to me, including a sonata in four bars, a symphony in three chords, and a song without words, in paraphrase of Mr. Spence's "fragment" in celebration of a night passed in the tomb. I was so thrilled and delighted by these selections that I quite forgot my perplexities, and revelled in the enjoyment of these new-found theories. Presently too Miss Kingsley came over to sit by me, radiant and expressive as before. The coolness on her part had completely vanished, and needless to say my heart felt lighter.

Resolving to be natural and to obtain as much benefit as possible from an opportunity that I might never have again, I moved about the room and managed to renew my conversation with Mr. Fleisch, who after a momentary coldness seemed gratified at my expressions of interest in his musical ideas. We recommenced the Economic system of speech, and presently were joined by Miss Kingsley. I rapidly grew proficient; and so absorbed did I become in an attempt made by us three to carry on connectedly an entire conversation in single words, that I was startled at hearing a voice just behind me say, —

" Carriage."

I turned, and found myself face to face with Mr. Spence. I understood that he had come to announce to me the arrival of my coupé.

" Servant," he added.

This told me that my maid was waiting at the door.

Mr. Spence's face was courteous but grave, and his lips were firmly set. During the time of my conversation with Mr. Fleisch and Miss Kingsley he had been sitting apart with Mrs. Marsh, while Paul Barr had returned to the piano and played a series of passionate and ardent music, the words of which he sung in a deep bass. But at the knock of my maid he paused, and now sat looking back over his shoulder at me with pathetic eyes.

" Home," I said to my hostess.

" Early."

" Horses."

" Sorry."

Her face expressed the regret at my departure which it seemed to me any extra words would have impaired the artistic value of, so much of a convert to the views regarding moderation had I become.

Miss Kingsley produced my wraps from her boudoir, which Paul Barr with a brace of sighs assisted me to put on. I bade good evening to them all. Mr. Spence made me a low but formal bow. I could see his lip tremble. The instant after, as with Paul Barr at my side I began to descend the stairs, a hurried step behind told me that the master was coming also. I went down to my carriage with one on either hand, the artist-poet pouring out a flood of words which I scarcely heeded, while Mr. Spence in an occasional monosyllable endeavored to express the hope that he might meet me again.

Just as I reached the threshold a superb rose, which had been the only ornament of my costume, chanced to fall from my corsage on the marble floor. It lay nearest to Mr. Spence, who started to pick it up. But he hesitated, and the consequent delay was taken advantage of by his rival, who had darted forward at the same moment. Mr. Barr lifted the rose and pressed it to his lips eagerly, twice and thrice. Then, without asking my leave, he put it in his button-hole. It was he too who helped me into my carriage. He bent low over the hand I gave him, while Mr. Spence, still irresolute, bowed from the shadow of the doorway.

"May I have the honor of calling upon you?" asked Paul Barr.

"Certainly, if you wish. And, Mr. Spence, I shall be very glad to see you also," I cried from the carriage window.

IV.

I FELT next morning a little as if my experience of the previous night were a dream. But as I thought over all that had occurred, what may be called the romantic features seemed to dwindle in distinctness and importance, and I dwelt chiefly on the mental profit I had derived from these new associations. Once more I deplored the existence of the vain and coquettish notions that had led me to construe as devotion the enthusiasm of the clever men who had honored me with an explanation of their original and interesting conceptions. It was clear that I was still not wholly free from flippancy and nonsense.

I did not attempt to decide between the merits of the diametrically opposed schools of thought represented by Mr. Spence and Mr. Barr. I was sensible enough to understand that long study and reflection would be requisite to qualify me to take sides intelligently. But yet I had already a distinct preference. I felt that whatever the value of his system, Mr. Spence was thoroughly and grandly in earnest. His whole soul was in the spread and development of his peculiar doctrines. To obtain their recognition he was willing to sacrifice luxury, comfort, and all the pleasures of life. Everything else was a secondary consideration. Already in the course of his thorough investigations he had endured horrors and committed extravagances from which a nature so palpably refined as his must have shrunk with loathing. It was novel and delightful to me to meet a man so completely absorbed in a pursuit which promised no reward beyond the amelioration of society, — a result of which he could hope to live to see only the beginnings. For mere dollars and cents he cared nothing. He had no ambition to grow rich; indeed, it was one of his tenets that no one should retain more than a certain amount of property, — doubtless enough to keep the wolf from the door, and to permit the continuation of scholarship. How much more unselfish and ennobling a life than that of the feverish money-getter, with all his appliances of forge and factory, and export and import! I had found an answer to my yearnings and my unrest in this untiring devotion to abstract truth.

A part of this was true undoubtedly of Paul Barr as well. Ardor and zeal were the very essence of his philosophy; but it was easy to divine by looking at him — at least it appeared so to me — that he lacked the spirit of persistent, unselfish scholarship which distinguished his rival. I felt that he was superficial, and that he would rather sacrifice his principles than his own interests.

All the more did I have faith in this instinctive preference for Mr. Spence, from the fact that from the standpoint of the picturesque and romantic everything was on the side of the artist-poet. Tall, dashing, handsome, and brilliant, he was adapted and doubtless accustomed to carry hearts by storm. No woman could receive his admiring glances without that slight thrill and flutter of the heart which proves the presence of a fascinating man. On the other hand the master — I liked to think of him as such — was, as I have already intimated, commonplace in appearance at the first glance, and save for his marvellous voice distinguished for none of those graces which attract my sex. Perhaps it would be more just to say that he sought to repress them rather than that they did not exist, for when under the influence of enthusiasm for his science his face was inspiring to look upon.

Such were the conclusions at which I arrived after sifting my impressions. But never did my incapacity and dearth of knowledge appear to me in a less complimentary light than at this time. I vowed again and again to give myself up unreservedly to study, and first of all to choose some special branch that would prevent my efforts from resulting in merely desultory work. If so, what better field could I choose than that in which there were fellow-workers already whom I knew, and with whom I could sympathize? The more I thought about the subject the stronger did the argument in favor of this selection appear. At last one morning in an access of enthusiasm I sat down and wrote a note to Mr. Spence, asking if he would be kind enough to call on me at his leisure,— "on a matter of business," I added, so as to preclude any possible misinterpretation on his part.

This was about a week after Miss Kingsley's tea. In the mean time I had been to see Aunt Agnes twice, but had not found her at home. I was curious to hear what Miss Kingsley would say concerning me, for I felt by no means sure that her remarks would be wholly complimentary. Freely as I blamed myself for my conceited notions at the time, regarding the attentions of the two philosophers, I was not ready to absolve her from the imputation of jealousy. It was difficult to explain her conduct on any other ground, and I remembered what Mrs. Marsh had said as to tender relations between her and Mr. Spence. Indeed, I felt some irritation against her and a conviction that she was not likely to be altogether my friend when we were not face to face. However, she had chosen to insert my name in the next issue of the "Mercury" as having been present at a small gathering at her "parlors" to meet "the distinguished scientist and poet, Charles Liversage Spence,"—a notice which she doubtless considered " sympathetic."

I stayed at home the whole of the day following that on which I wrote to Mr. Spence, and was rewarded by receiving a visit from him in the afternoon. He seemed little at his ease when he entered the room, and I observed a number of details of dress and manner which showed that he was not versed in the usages of fashionable life despite his early experiences. These lapses, or rather differences, did not affect me disagreeably,—indeed, I was well content that he should be as unlike as possible the flippant youths of so-called society,—but they were much more noticeable than when he was in the midst of such artistic surroundings as he found at Miss Kingsley's.

I judged it best to enter at once on the matter I had at heart.

"You will pardon me I am sure, Mr. Spence, for taking up your valuable time, when I tell you my reason for asking you to call upon me. I will be frank, and say that I have been for some time anxious to find an interest to which I could devote myself thoroughly and systematically, and one that was wholly in sympathy with what I feel to be my tastes and aspirations. I have a great deal of time at my disposal, and have become weary of the amusements of society and of the merely superficial character of my studies hitherto. The exercises to which I had the good fortune to listen at Miss Kingsley's the other evening were almost a revelation to me. They confirmed at least the opinion I had begun to have, that outside of what the world calls fashionable circles there is a class of people who like yourself find their happiness in intellectual aims and pleasures. So much interested was I by what I heard then, that I have decided, after some hesitation on the score of troubling you, to offer myself as a student of your system of

Moderation. It may be," I added, speaking hurriedly in my desire to put the matter clearly before him, and yet not to be prolix, "you do not care for the co-operation of persons so little advanced as I; for I tell you honestly that though tolerably proficient in what are known as accomplishments, I am ignorant of all that appertains to serious knowledge. But believe me when I say that I am thorougly in earnest, and will devote myself to the cause with all my heart, in case you think me able to be of assistance."

Mr. Spence heard me to the end without interruption. I had looked straight before me, intent alone upon presenting my case in such a light that while he knew the worst, he would not reject my request to become one of his pupils. Nor did he reply at once. I glanced at him, and saw that he was blushing; but he mastered his confusion, and said quietly: —

"Miss Harlan, I have received few compliments in my life more acceptable than that comprised in what you have just said to me. It is precisely to such alert and reflective minds as yours that I wish to make my theories interesting. I am devoting the sum of my energies to the propagation of what I regard as a truth vital to the well-being of humanity. You know the leading features of my system already. I will not disguise from you that an advocacy of them will expose you to publicity, it may be to ridicule. Our converts are as yet few; and in order to be of service, those who devote themselves to the work must be enthusiastic. I do not say this because I doubt your sincerity or steadfastness; probably you have considered these things already. But it is right that you should be fully informed regarding the character of the cause you propose to adopt."

"But I may decide not to adopt it in the end, Mr. Spence," I said, not wishing to commit myself irrevocably. "I am very much interested in your ideas, but I should prefer to be accepted merely as a student until I am more familiar with them. As I have said, I am very ignorant of all such matters, and need instruction. I have spoken to you rather to ask your advice as to whom to select as a teacher, than to offer myself as an active convert. The rest will come in time, I have no doubt, for I am greatly attracted by what I have heard already."

"I see. You are right," said he. "Precipitation is directly opposed to the spirit of my theories. I should have said you were already qualified to become an active worker, but you are the best judge: and, as you have mentioned, you will be able to become familiar with the system at your leisure."

He paused, and seemed to be absorbed in thought, as though he were debating with himself.

"Do you know of any good teacher?" I inquired.

"I am reflecting."

"I should expect to pay any competent person liberally."

He flushed a little, and after an instant said:

"I thought at first that I might see my way to offering myself as an instructor, but on reflection I find it would be difficult for me to find time. I know of no better persons to suggest than one of our friends of the other evening,— Mr. Fleisch or Miss Kingsley. Either of them is admirably well informed and intelligent."

"Oh, but if you could arrange it so, I should much prefer you, Mr. Spence," I exclaimed with genuine eagerness. "I did not dare to imagine that such an arrangement was possible. But now that you have suggested it yourself, I cannot give up the idea without remonstrance."

I looked at him beseechingly, and he blushed again in a manner to cause me self-consciousness.

He hesitated, and then in a decided tone, as if he were resisting a temptation, said: —

"It is out of the question, Miss Harlan. I have not time. Mr. Fleisch is an excellent instructor."

"Very well; Mr. Fleisch then," I answered, a little upset by his confusion. "Will you speak to him about it and arrange the terms?"

He assented, and the awkward pause that followed was relieved by the entrance, at the same moment, of Aunt Helen and Mr. Barr, though not in company it need scarcely be added.

Aunt Helen was in one of her richest and most imposing street costumes, whereas the artist-poet wore black velveteen instead of brown, and a flowing yellow tie instead of a cherry one. She regarded him, I could see, with a mixture of horror and wonder, which led me at once to perform the duties of a general introduction, preliminary to taking possession of Mr. Barr, and relegating to Aunt Helen the less unconventional philosopher. Paul Barr however bowed to her in so superb and deferential a manner that I thought she looked rather flattered than otherwise, which relieved my worst apprehensions, and I found myself straightway chatting with him in a somewhat spirited vein. Heard, in my own drawing-room, Mr. Barr's compliments and ardent speeches moved me to badinage, and I saw no harm in accepting them as the ordinary give-and-take of the would-be lady-killer, more original and therefore more entertaining than those of a fashionable flirt, but still of the same general character. I affected to be alternately irate and pleased at what he said. Meanwhile his eyes looked unutterable things, and he interspersed his flatteries with a tissue of abnormal but poetic fancies. He was undeniably fascinating, and all the more so because I felt in his society somewhat as if I were walking through a gunpowder vault, with a lighted candle. But there was this difference, that in his case the character of the possible explosion was wrapped in mysterious uncertainty, which added an agreeable element of curiosity to my sensations.

Presently he drew from his breast pocket a small volume in white vellum and gold, which he presented to me. It was a copy of his poems, — "The Paradise of Passion, and other Rhythms." I glanced at the fly-leaf, and to my astonishment and confusion perceived that underneath the inscription, " Miss Harlan, with the respectful homage of him who did these verses," was a sonnet "To Virginia," which began, —

> The happy rose which lately from thy hands
> I took with kisses, dry and withered lies —

I did not attempt to read farther at the moment. Indeed, I felt inclined to draw myself up austerely at first, but on second thought acknowledged his presumption with the same laughing coquetry I had hitherto displayed. After all, it was not worth while to become angry. His extravagance was not to be taken too seriously. It was rather refreshing for a change. I wondered how he would behave if he ever really were in love.

Meanwhile I had endeavored to listen at the same time to the conversation between Aunt Helen and Mr. Spence. I was relieved to find that he saw fit to avoid any allusion to his theories, and pursued the highway of indifferent subjects, such as the weather, the stage, and foreign travel. Still, I could tell from Aunt Helen's superior and as it seemed to me disdainful tone that she by no means approved of my new acquaintances, though I detected her casting an occasional glance of puzzled curiosity at Mr. Barr, whose eccentricities were,

I suppose, more amusing than the calm of her companion.

"I don't suppose you find the differences very marked between this country and Europe, Mr. Spence?" I heard her inquire after learning that he had passed much of his life abroad.

"On the contrary, very slight."

"Nice people are very much the same everywhere," she observed haughtily.

"To tell the truth," said Mr. Spence, "I have been rather disappointed at finding the people, as well as the manners and customs, of this country so similar to those across the water. I had been led to expect originality and independence. That was what I was taught to believe as a child. But after an absence from my country of six years I came back to find nearly the same manners and customs, and the same virtues and vices, as I left behind me in Europe."

"Vices?" echoed Aunt Helen. "I should say there was much less vice in this country than in Europe."

"Not if we judge by the newspapers."

"Ah, but one can't believe all one reads in the newspapers," she said with an air of triumph.

Mr. Spence had, unluckily for the impression he was likely to create, the courage of his convictions as I well knew, and as he began to reply I felt less secure that he would not trench upon dangerous ground.

"There is a general tendency to ape foreign ideas, which is fast destroying our originality as a nation," he continued.

"Foreign ideas are often the best," said my aunt.

"We are beginning to talk and dress, and dine and give in marriage, just like all the rest of the world," he explained, without regarding her comment.

Aunt Helen looked a little blank. Then with her most stately air she said:—

"Surely you would n't have marriages performed before a Justice of the Peace? It destroys all their sentiment. I know a great many persons who would n't consider themselves married so. As to living differently, I don't know what you mean. There are people here who advocate cremation, co-operation, and that sort of thing, but one does n't meet them in society."

"I am no judge," said Mr. Spence coolly, "for I never go into society."

"Indeed!" Aunt Helen surveyed him through her eye-glass as if he were a curious animal, and her haughtiness perceptibly increased. "Are you — eh — in business in Boston?"

"No, madam. I am a Bohemian," replied Mr. Spence, in whose eye I perceived a twinkle.

"A what? Ah, yes, of course. I understood you to say you were born in this country. And the other gentleman — eh — is he a foreigner too?"

For an instant Mr. Spence looked bewildered; and as for me I was inwardly convulsed, so much so that I betrayed my feelings in a smile at the moment when Paul Barr was reciting a blood-curdling piece of poetry of his own composing, — an indiscretion which offended the artist-poet to such an extent that in my efforts to mollify him I failed to catch Mr. Spence's reply. He rose to take his leave at this point; but it chanced that just then my father entered the room, and I was obliged to repeat the introductions. While I was saying a few last words to Mr. Spence in regard to the sort of instruction I was to receive from Mr. Fleisch, Paul Barr conversed with my father, laying down the law in his most superb fashion regarding the immense fortune in store for any one who would start what he called a fig farm in this country. Although I had never heard him broach a business matter before, he seemed entirely familiar with his subject, and fairly bristled with statistics and calculations to prove the soundness of his theory, gardeners to the contrary notwithstanding. My father listened to him patiently, and seemed to be amused. Aunt Helen sat apart with a reserved, patrician air.

My two callers took their leave together; and when the front door closed, my father said jocosely, —

"Who are your friends, Virginia? I hope they have not been persuading you to invest in a fig farm."

I blushed, remembering my former design of speculating with Mr. Dale, — of which, however, my father had no knowledge.

"Both are literary men of high reputation," I answered quietly, though I had an instinctive feeling that my father would make sport of this assertion. But experience had taught me that with him it was best to call a spade a spade.

"That accounts for it. I thought the gentleman in velveteen had a screw loose somewhere," he said as he passed out of the room.

"Well, Virginia," exclaimed Aunt Helen when we were alone, " whom *have* you picked up now?"

"I don't understand you," said I.

"Who are those young men who were here just now? They are foreigners, on their own admission, — Bohemians. My own belief is that they have gypsy blood in their veins, for what can one know of the antecedents of persons who come from a small German principality? They don't even claim to be counts, and any one with the smallest pretext to respectability in that part of the world is a count, at least. They look to me as if they had been on the stage, especially the one to whom you were talking. I will do him the justice to say he is a handsome wretch, but like all those foreign adventurers he has a dissipated air. As for the other, he is simply commonplace and vulgar, with little upstart radical notions."

I waited for her to finish before replying. "I have already said that Mr. Spence and Mr. Barr are both literary men of high standing. They are neither of them foreigners, but were born in this State. By 'Bohemian' Mr. Spence meant the literary and artistic fraternity in general, Aunt Helen. He is a philosopher as well as a poet; and Mr. Barr paints pictures in addition to his other work."

"But who are they? Where do they come

from? It is all very well to say they were born in this country. But who and what are their parents? Spence — Spence — I never heard the name in my life. There were some Barrs who used to live in the next street to us when your mother and I were young; but they were all girls, and, as I remember them, ordinary."

"When men have acquired fame, it is hardly necessary to inquire if they belong to the best families," I rejoined, borrowing a leaf from Aunt Agnes's book.

"It is one thing to admire the works of genius, and another to have it trampoosing over your house. Your acquaintances are, I dare say, well enough as poets and philosophers, but I don't see what that has to do with you. You are neither a poet nor a philosopher, and you will flatter them much more by buying their books than by asking them to five o'clock tea. I must say that, philosopher or no philosopher, the young man who was talking with me has very strange ideas. Just think of his advocating co-operative house-keeping, and marriages before a Justice of the Peace. I fancy too that he is lax in his religious opinions. If he is your idea of a desirable acquaintance to invite to your house,

I am sorry for it. You never got any such notions from my side of the family."

"It is useless to talk with you if you go off at a tangent, Aunt Helen," said I. "I am proud to call both those young men my friends, and they are vastly superior in every way to nine tenths of those one meets in society. Mr. Spence, whose ideas you think so peculiar, is one of the ablest scientists in the country, and I am going to take lessons in his philosophy from one of his assistants. As I told you the other day, I am tired of frittering away my time in nonsense."

"And as I told *you* the other day, Virginia, go on as you have begun, and we shall hear of you presently on the stage. That Mr. Barr might pass in a drawing-room on account of his picturesqueness, if he were to brush his hair; but the other one is simply a gawk, to be plain. Science indeed! Don't come in a few weeks to ask me to believe that we are all descended from monkeys, or any other stuff, for I sha'n't do it. That's what I call nonsense; and you will discover some day that most people who have any self-respect are of my way of thinking."

I had never known Aunt Helen to be so excited, but there was nothing to be done. Society and etiquette were her household gods; and by ceasing to worship the same divinities I had drawn upon myself the full energy of her displeasure. Nothing could have offended her so much. To be odd or different from other people was in her estimation a cardinal sin; whereas I parted from her with a still firmer conviction that I had chosen wisely. The calm unselfish wisdom and steadfastness of Mr. Spence seemed more indisputable to me than ever; and in the way of companionship, Paul Barr's gallantries and sallies were vastly preferable to any drawing-room flirtation.

It was only when I thought of my father that I felt any concern or doubt. I knew that he had set his heart upon my devoting myself to the study of practical matters. He wished me to become cultivated, but scarcely in the direction I had chosen. What would he say if he knew of my determination; and was it filial and just to let him remain in ignorance of it? Yet I reasoned that after all I had made no final decision. I was attracted, it is true, by what might be called a visionary theory; but when I had given the principles of moderation further thought, I might conclude not to devote myself to them. It would be time enough later to speak of the subject. At present I was only too poorly prepared to present the ideas of Mr. Spence in an intelligent manner, and should probably prejudice my father against the whole system.

However, I could not refrain from a few reflections on the apparent hostility of practical men to pure theory, which must after all be the basis of all intelligent action. How much nobler to help to establish principles serviceable to humanity than to make later unconscious use of those same principles to advance one's own selfish interests! Why must there needs be mutual disdain and coolness between those who thought and those who acted? It had been easy for me to perceive at a glance that there was likely to be but little mutual sympathy between my father and Mr. Spence, and the consciousness grieved me.

But I did not falter in my purpose. Mr. Fleisch called to see me the following day and laid out an elaborate course of study. He was to come twice a week to examine me and give me suggestions, but he said that my progress was mainly dependent on my own exertions. I bought a number of books of his selection, and tried to devote five hours each day to systematic work.

My tasks were largely of a philosophical character, but poetry and music of a restrained sort were also included in Mr. Fleisch's instruction; and he said that after the foundations were laid, I should be taught the dangers of extremes by studying examples of the overmuch and the undermuch.

At last I was successful one day in finding Aunt Agnes at home, and alone. It was about a week after my visit from Mr. Spence. I was disturbed at seeing her brow contract at sight of me, but my worst fears were realized when she said: —

"I do not wonder that you have preferred to keep away from me."

"On the contrary, Aunt Agnes, I have called twice before, this week."

"When you knew I was out, I dare say."

There was no answering such logic as this.

"I seem never to be able to satisfy you," I said bravely. "I had come to tell you that I am studying hard under the direction of Mr. Fleisch, a favorite pupil of Mr. Spence, and am doing all I can to improve myself."

"Fiddlesticks! Tell *me!*"

"But, Aunt Agnes, it is so."

"I have heard all about you. You can't tell

me anything about the matter I don't know already. We shall hear next of your carrying your habit of flirting into the sanctuary itself. You might almost as well coquet with a minister of the holy Gospel as with him you have selected to try your fascinations on. I might have guessed what would be the result of introducing you to sober-minded people. It was none of my work, thank Heaven! Lucretia Kingsley has herself to blame, for I heard her give you the invitation from her own lips. But I blush for you as my niece. No amount of proficiency or cleverness can be a palliation of your behavior."

"I have been maligned, Aunt Agnes," I cried with flashing eyes. "Some one has told you a pack of falsehoods. It is not true that I have been flirting with anybody. I have given up everything of the kind, as I said I should. Who has been accusing me? I insist on knowing who told you."

"No matter who told me. My authority is of the best."

"I suppose it was your friend Miss Kingsley. I half suspected that she would misrepresent me In private."

"You admit, then, that you are guilty?"

"I admit nothing. If, as your words seem to imply, Miss Kingsley says I acted unbecomingly at her house, she does not speak the truth. She is jealous. The long and short of it is, Mr. Spence was polite to me, and that made her angry. I believe she wishes to marry him herself," I said in the fulness of my anger.

"Virginia! I am astonished at you. It will not mend matters to insult your benefactors. What motive had Miss Kingsley, pray, in asking you to her house but kindness?"

"Pshaw!" I cried, now thoroughly roused. "She asked me because she thought I was fashionable, and because it would read well in the newspaper that I had been at one of her tea-parties. She imagined I was so silly and brainless that her friends would take no notice of me; and when it turned out that they did she lost her temper."

"You have lost yours, Virginia. I presume you will tell me presently that Mr. Spence flirted with you. I never heard such nonsense in my life, and wicked nonsense too; for you are doing your best to injure the character of a young woman who is in every way your superior, and has had none of your advantages. As I just said, I presume you will claim that Mr. Spence flirted with you, and that he wrote to you first."

"Wrote to me? He has never written to me; nor I to him, except to ask his advice about a teacher."

"You admit so much?"

"Why shouldn't I? I was interested in his theories, and I applied to him as the most natural person to consult."

"It is very easy to explain it away in that manner, but unfortunately for you my informant adopted —"

"Why don't you say Miss Kingsley, and have done with it, Aunt Agnes?"

"Very well then, if you prefer, Miss Kingsley adopted a very different style in speaking of you than you employ in speaking of her. She tried to spare you as much as possible, and said what she did only with great reluctance. I could see that she was holding back, and was resolved not to tell the whole. 'Of course,' she said, 'I know Miss Virginia did not mean to offend, and very likely in general society her little indiscretions would have been quite proper; but at a purely intellectual gathering like ours, from which as you know all vanities are rigorously excluded, it did seem to me unsympathetic of a new-comer to introduce an element of coquetry When I say that since then she has written notes to Mr. Spence, whose time is precious as gold, asking him to call upon her in a social way, you will I am sure, my dear Miss Harlan, excuse my speaking. It is for her own good that I have ventured to do so, as a word from you would convince her of her thoughtlessness.'"

"The hypocrite!" I murmured, too indignant to restrain myself.

"There you go again, vilifying her with abusive epithets when she has simply done her duty as a friend. Contrast for instance your various expressions with hers. 'Jealous;' 'invited you to her house because you were fashionable' (a most unwarranted assumption); 'a hypocrite;' and, worst of all, you accuse her of trying to win the affections of a man whom she venerates as a master, and who though he has never taken the vow of celibacy is too much absorbed in the life-work he is pursuing to give a thought to marriage. And what does she say of you? She merely calls it 'unsympathetic' of a new-comer to disturb the harmony of sober-minded people by the introduction of coquetry. 'Unsympathetic'! If I were to stigmatize such behavior, I should call it disgraceful.

I was mortified, Virginia, thoroughly mortified; and especially as Mr. Spence had been here the day before, and spoken of you in terms that made me feel really proud. As Miss Kingsley said, however, he is the last man in the world to notice such a thing as coquetry."

I made a mental interrogation point, but I did not dare to give utterance to the heresy lest I should seem to be carrying out Aunt Agnes's insinuation that I would next accuse Mr. Spence of flirting with me. I replied with as much quietness as I could at the moment command, —

"I can only repeat what I have already said. Miss Kingsley has slandered me, whether intentionally or not I do not know. But her charge of coquetry is utterly without foundation."

"Did you not make eyes at Mr. Barr, and give him a rose?" she interrupted. "You see I know all."

"No, I did not," I answered, flushing. "On the contrary, Mr. Barr made me feel excessively uncomfortable during most of the evening by the absurd compliments he paid me, and by the way in which he stared at me. As for the rose, I dropped it accidentally as I was getting into my carriage, and I believe he picked it up."

"Accidentally!" said Aunt Agnes with a sniff.

"As my informant said, 'when a young woman flings herself at the head of a hot-souled poet, what is she to expect?' Human nature is human nature, and there are not many men with the self-control of Mr. Spence."

"Miss Kingsley seems to have given you a great deal of information, Aunt Agnes."

"You are mistaken again, as usual. The person who told me this is a sober-minded woman of middle age, who could not have been influenced by jealousy."

"Mrs. Marsh, I suppose. I might have known it, from her choice vocabulary. Talk of gossips, Aunt Agnes, I never heard a worse one in any drawing-room in the city. Who *is* Mrs Marsh?"

I was glowing with indignation again, and justly so as it seemed to me. I had been cruelly misconstrued, and my self-control on the occasion of Miss Kingsley's tea had been wholly unappreciated.

"Who is Mrs. Marsh? You may well ask who is Mrs. Marsh, after what you have said about her. Gossip or no gossip, vocabulary or no vocabulary, Mrs. Marsh is a very deserving woman, who by her own unaided efforts has risen to the position she now occupies. How often shall I be obliged to impress upon you that it is the spirit, not the letter, that is of importance? As secretary of the Society for the Practice of Moderation, Mrs Marsh can afford to disregard the ill-natured sneers of those who may have enjoyed greater advantages in early life than she. It is not by wholesale abuse of others, Virginia, that you will persuade me of your innocence. On your own showing, you have written to Mr. Spence, and misconstrued Mr. Barr's poetic impetuosity as an attempt to flirt with you. I do not desire to discuss the matter further. We shall soon know whether you are sincere or not in your professions of study. As I have told you before, your future is in your own hands; but first and foremost you must rid yourself of this propensity to behave in a trivial manner."

I felt that silence would be the best palliative for my wounds; and so discouraged was I of being able to change Aunt Agnes's opinion, I thought it a waste of breath at the moment even to mention Mrs. Marsh as my authority for the statement that Miss Kingsley had a tender feeling for Mr. Spence.

V.

A YEAR passed without special incident, and yet certain things require to be told so that the sequel may seem consistent. Contrary to Aunt Agnes's insinuation, I proved sincere in my devotion to study. Mr. Fleisch came regularly twice a week, and during the summer months when I was away from home his instruction was continued by means of correspondence. I found him, as Mr. Spence had predicted, an admirable teacher. His work was everything to him, and he imbued me with his ability to look at our relations as strictly impersonal. He might have been a machine, so little was he susceptible to any mood of mine, — a characteristic which I deemed more and more indispensable each day to a proper understanding between pupil and master.

As a result of his teaching and my own industry, I acquired before many months an intimate knowledge of the views shared by those who called themselves Moderationists, and moreover without the slightest diminution of my enthusiasm. I was able to converse intelligently with the most proficient of the school, and there was little of the system that failed to commend itself to me as entitled to faith and support. I attended meetings and lectures in advocacy of its theories, and occasionally took part in debates on questions relating to the management of the Society for the Practice of Moderation, of which I was elected treasurer. Thus it happened that my name appeared in the newspapers as one of the leading spirits of the movement, and among my former acquaintances there was a general impression that I had become very peculiar. My old ball-room rivals, who were for the most part waltzing as hard as ever, would stop me in the street and say, "Virginia dear, is it true you are going into a convent?" or, "What is this that I hear, Virginia, about you being in favor of female suffrage? Do you really think women ought to vote?" Once in a while some friend, who was either more accurate by nature or who really felt an interest in me, would hit closer to the mark, and perhaps with a sigh express regret at not having the courage to become literary too. "But it does separate one so from other people,—that is, people one knows; don't you think so dear?"

It certainly did. I was completely estranged from my old associations, and spent my time, when not employed in study, largely at the rooms of our Society, where Mrs. Marsh presided as secretary. There were countless circulars and pamphlets to be mailed, setting forth our purposes and needs. Mrs. Marsh, despite an inaccurate acquaintance with and an overweening curiosity regarding the doings of fashionable people, was a model of executive ability. With some one at hand to correct her grammar and spelling, she could transact a greater amount of business than half-a-dozen ordinary women. In my zeal to see things properly done, I constituted myself her assistant; and we managed together the whole work of the Bureau, as Miss Kingsley liked to call our humble quarters.

My relations with Miss Kingsley were outwardly very friendly. I had thought it best upon reflection not to appear offended when we met again, and she on her part greeted me with effusive warmth and a little deprecatory look, as if to say, "You will excuse me, I am sure, for what I said to your aunt. It was for your good, or I should never have spoken." Subsequently, in our relations at the Bureau, she liked to patronize me slightly. She would come whisking into the rooms where Mrs. Marsh and I were hard at work, and putter about for a few moments, asking questions and giving us advice, and then whisk out again with an encouraging nod. She was apt to time her visits so as to meet Mr. Spence, who came regularly sometime during every forenoon, to superintend our labors. He stayed usually about half an hour; and from the first day I became connected with the Bureau I made a point to avoid him as much as possible, — a course which seemed acceptable to him, for he always addressed his business suggestions to Mrs. Marsh, and did not encourage me to converse with him. Once in a while, however, he would approach me in a constrained fashion, and express satisfaction with the reports Mr. Fleisch made of my progress. It was through his silent agency also, I had no question, that I was appointed treasurer, and was regarded as a prominent worker in the cause. With Miss Kingsley, on the other hand, he was easy and familiar. It was evident that he liked her, and he listened to her opinions; but I could never detect what seemed to me any signs of sentiment on his part in her regard. Miss Kingsley must have thought differently, for on one or two occasions she was unable to resist the temptation, as they went out of the door together, of looking back at me with an air of triumph. The more Mr. Spence seemed to avoid me, the kinder and more patronizing was her manner; and she so far evinced her friendship presently as to show me the manuscript of a novel which she had written, entitled " Moderation," and which was dedicated " To him to whom I owe all that in me is of worth, — Charles Liversage Spence." It was an attempt, as she explained to me, to return to the rational style and improving tone of Jane Austen, whose novels were sound educators as well as sources of amusement. From Miss Kingsley's natural fluency and sprightliness I expected something "racy," to quote Paul Barr, and I was disappointed to find " Moderation " dull and didactic. It was however heralded and published with a great flourish of trumpets; and Mr. Spence wrote a review of it in one of the leading newspapers under the symbol XXX (a signature of his known only to the initiated), in which he called attention to its exquisite moral tone, which had no counterpart in fiction since the writings of Miss Edgeworth were on every parlor table. In conclusion he said: " Whatever the too captious critic may say of the dramatic interest of the story, it is indeed a triumph for a young writer, and that writer a woman, to embody in her first novel opinions that will make the book of value to the student of psychology long after the craving of human nature for fictitious narrative has ceased to exist."

My own opinion of the novel was reinforced by that of Paul Barr, which prevented me from thinking, as I might otherwise have done, that I was actuated by ill-nature in judging Miss Kingsley's book. After the first phase of curiosity its popularity waned, and the author adopted the fashion of calling it an artistic success. But the complimentary criticism of Mr. Spence gave me food for thought, and for the first time suggested the idea of a possible feeling on his part for Miss Kingsley stronger than friendship. It interested me, and at the same time annoyed me a little. Why the latter I hardly knew, unless it were a conviction that she was not good enough for him. But when I thought over their daily relations as constantly exhibited in my presence, my former opinion that he had merely a brotherly affection for her returned. If he had been misled to praise her book unduly, it was by his excessive enthusiasm for his own doctrines presented therein, and not by the blind force of love,

— which conclusion was directly at variance with the theory of Mrs. Marsh on the subject, who was perpetually referring to the match between them as a foregone conclusion.

Discreet as was my conduct in general during these twelve months, and earnestly as I sought to avoid in its mildest form what Aunt Agnes called coquetry, I was not able to escape the importunities of Mr. Barr. Absorbed as I was in my work, and determined to consider all attentions from my literary friends as mere meaningless gallantries, it was very difficult to disregard the artist-poet's protestations of devotion: they had become little short of that. He was a constant visitor at the rooms of our Society, although his own principles were hostile to those we professed; and he would spend as much time as I would permit, lolling about my desk and whispering all sorts of nonsense. He brought me flowers and fruit, and now and then some new publication, — not in sufficient quantity to permit me to refuse them, but a single rose or a peach, or a tiny volume of verses. He sent me sonnets and madrigals through the post without signature, though in his own handwriting, and denied with asseverations their authorship when questioned. Besides his black and his brown, he had a green velveteen coat, and a different-colored flowing tie for every day in the week. His habits were in complete conformity with his philosophy of extremes. He was apt to tell me when he had been sitting up all night, whether in study or what he called wassail; but I could always guess the fact from his appearance. His method of work was equally irregular, and he lived from hand to mouth. He would be idle as a forced peach on a hot-house wall (to use a simile of his own) for weeks at a time; and yet when he was seized with a desire to work, it was no uncommon thing for him to paint or compose twenty-four hours at a sitting, and come to the Bureau or my house, almost before I was out of bed, with dishevelled raiment and bloodshot eyes, to exhibit or read to me the result of his industry.

I had by this time ceased to regard him with any seriousness as a philosopher. Indeed, it was difficult not to consider his vagaries self-indulgence; and from the veneration I conceived for him at the start, I came to be his mentor in the end. I dared to remonstrate with him on the irresponsible life he was leading, and sought to inculcate in him the doctrine of moderation. I felt that I had an influence over him; and it was the consciousness of this that prompted me not to be too severe in the matter of his attentions and little gifts. When I talked to him, as I often did, on the error of his ways and the waste of his talents, he would listen to me with tears in his eyes, and promise better things for the future. He would become systematic and serious in his habits and work. Without becoming a convert to moderation, he would develop his own scheme of philosophy in an artistic spirit. There was a limit even to extremes, he said; and that limit scientifically determined would induce a perfect happiness. When he talked thus, I felt I could afford to be indifferent to the insinuations and playful sallies of Miss Kingsley and Mrs. Marsh. They might think what they chose of our relations. If by the exercise of sympathy and counsel I could regenerate a man of strong individuality and striking natural gifts from the thrall of self-indulgence, a fig for the idle voice of gossip!

Meanwhile, I grieve to say that my intimacy with Aunt Helen was strained. Many were the tears she shed over my degeneracy, and no words of mine could make her see other than a foolish waste of golden opportunities in the course I was pursuing. This disturbed me greatly, for my attachment to her was very strong, and I knew she would have cut off her right hand to serve me. Our interviews were largely lachrymose on her part and morose on mine, after argument proved futile. She had none of Aunt Agnes's downrightness, but a no less degree of persistence. After many efforts, I succeeded in convincing her that my friends had no connection with the stage, and I persuaded her to accompany me to one of Mr. Spence's lectures. It was the one on Over-eating and Under-eating, and the most likely to be fully intelligible, I thought. But I caught her napping before the end; and as an all-embracing condemnatory criticism, she cautioned me to beware of homœopathy!

With Aunt Agnes, on the other hand, my relations were more friendly than they had ever been before. Experience had taught me that long conversations with her were not advisable, but I was able to test the thermometer of her feelings toward me in other ways. She had begun to send me books and pamphlets, relating to various abstract theories in which she was interested; and once or twice she read to me articles in manuscript of her own composition, and asked my opinion of their merit. Occasionally, too, she paid a visit to the rooms of the Society; and

I shall never forget the expression of satisfaction that flickered over her severe face at seeing me, for the first time, at my desk. From that day, a general softening of her attitude toward me began.

But happy and absorbed as I was in this great interest, I was never quite without a feeling that my father might not be pleased, did he know of my fast-growing intention to devote the energies of my life to it. He was more busy than ever down town, and for weeks at a time would seem scarcely aware of my existence. His questions at dinner regarding my doings were rarely more definite than to ask how I had spent the day, to which any reply seemed to be satisfactory. I usually said that I had been studying; and had it not been for his quiet habit of observation, with which I was now acquainted, I should have imagined that it went in at one ear and out at the other. I never volunteered to tell him the character of my studies; but though he never made inquiries, I had a secret impression that he knew far more than was apparent of the use I made of my time. Nevertheless, the year passed without his showing any signs of disapproval. I was so bold even as to invite Paul Barr once or twice to dinner, when I felt that he needed the moral tonic of a glimpse of home life to fortify his good resolutions. So, too, I did not hesitate to practise in my daily mode of living some of the doctrines to which I held most firmly, — such as early hours of rising and going to bed, temperate diet and simplicity of raiment; but as it was just as incumbent upon me to avoid the other extreme, the changes were not sufficiently marked to excite attention.

The traveller who looks back at night upon a highway sees a long trail of shadow, broken at recurring intervals by the blaze of lamps. Such is the effect of life in retrospect. Much of that which we remember concerning the past is vague and dim, yet here and there along the road some incident stands out which explains and illumines what follows and precedes.

It is difficult for me to analyze more closely than I have done my feelings and thoughts during the period in which I studied the principles of moderation. But the events of three days at its close are indelibly impressed upon my memory. For several weeks during the autumn, Paul Barr had been hard at work upon a picture in regard to which he had seen fit to be mysterious, although he became enthusiastic as to its merits before it was nearly finished. No piece of painting that he had ever attempted was so satisfactory to him, he said, both in the way of conception and performance. So confident was he of its excellence, that I began at last to share his excitement, and expressed a wish to see the masterpiece. But he was resolute in his determination that no one should see it until its completion, and least of all I.

Curious as I felt concerning it, — for one could never be sure that Paul Barr was not a genius, — I was in no haste to have the picture finished, for the artist's own sake. So deep and breathless was his interest, that he had become regular in his hours and habits. He seemed to realize that the best work required a steady hand and an unwearied eye. If I took some slight credit to myself for this change in his methods, it was not unnatural; and yet I was not so far elated as to feel wholly confident it would last. When he had put the finishing touch to his wonderful creation, would he abstain from the dissipation and self-indulgent idleness that was apt to follow any concentration on his part? I liked to believe that this would be the case; and as I cherished the idea, it grew almost into absolute faith.

I have said that Aunt Agnes and I were on pleasant terms; but there was one speck on the mirror of her serenity which threatened at times to mar the whole. It was my intimacy with Mr. Barr. Some one had informed her, — I have no doubt it was Miss Kingsley, — that he was much in my society, and that we behaved like lovers. I had learned by this time not to allow my awe for Aunt Agnes to prevent me from defending myself; but I found exculpation a difficult matter in this instance, on account of the character of the other offender. She styled my attitude hypocritical, because I parleyed with the enemy. Even assuming that there was no flirtation between us, — of which she was by no means convinced, — what right, she asked, had I, as a neophyte of recent standing, to be on terms of intimacy with the arch advocate of the school of thought most opposed to that which I professed?

I mention this in order to explain why I had of late been more chary of my sympathy in my interviews with the artist, and had given him strict orders that he was not to send me any more fruit and flowers. However much I might desire his welfare, self-respect required that I should not let our friendship become so conspicuous as to attract general attention. It was shortly after I issued this mandate that he began the picture to which I have referred; but the immediate result of my words was a fit of angry despondency.

Two days before Christmas he came to me and said the picture would be finished and ready for exhibition on Christmas Eve, and that he wished me to see it first of all. Would I come to his rooms on that afternoon? As he saw me hesitate, he clasped his hands with so piteous an expression that I chose not to say no. Why not, after all, thought I. It was unconventional to be sure. But matrons were out of date and superfluous in the artistic world. Did not Miss Kingsley go about freely to studios and wherever the needs of her profession called her? If she were safe from familiarity, why should not I be? I had a strong belief in the magic circle of respect which surrounds a thoroughly refined woman. If I refused the artist's request, I was certain to disappoint him sorely. It was a small enough favor, I argued, to grant to one who had been striving bravely to overcome his evil nature at my instigation.

Mr. Barr's studio was up seven flights of stairs in the French roof of a building which had no elevator, and had doubtless been chosen by him on account of cheapness and light. Breathless,

I paused on the last landing on the afternoon of the day before Christmas, and in response to my knock was greeted by the black beard and large eyes of the artist appearing round the edge of the door. As he threw it wide open he gave a cry of pleasure, singing the while at the top of his lungs the air he played that evening at Miss Kingsley's when he flung himself down before the piano after tea.

"At last, at last, my goddess! I have prayed for this hour," he said, bowing low.

I stopped short in the middle of the room. "If you do not wish me to leave you instantly, you must cease all such language and unseemly conduct. I have come to see your picture, Mr. Barr."

"I will. Believe me, I will. I will be quiet as a lamb, though I am so happy I could dance a minuet with Satan and not tire. But I will obey you. Do not be uneasy. Sit here. No, here. The light is better. There it is. Look, finished! My masterpiece, my ideal! It is only to lift that curtain, and I shall be famous."

Despite his words he was jumping about with nervous, excited gestures. I sat in the armchair he had indicated, and looked from him to the picture on the easel over which a drapery was flung, and back again to him. For an indefinable feeling of dread was coming over me, as I noted the disordered dress and the blood-shot eyes of my strange host. He had failed, then, to keep his pledges; had yielded to temptation. My hoped-for regeneration was a failure, and all was as it used to be with him. But yet it might be overwork and the strain of a night without sleep that gave him such a dissipated aspect. I tried to think it was so. Meanwhile he had seated himself at an old worn-out piano, and looking across to me was pounding out bar after bar of passionate music.

"Really, this is too much! I cannot stay and endure this absurdity," I cried, and I walked to the door.

But he darted at me and seized my hand with fierceness and the grip of a vice, so that I shook with fear.

"You shall not go, not until you have seen her, — her I adore. Sit there!" he thundered; and then, with an apparent sense of his own harshness, he fell on his knees before me and kissed my fingers with feverish frenzy. "My queen! my own!" he cried.

I was so frightened I could not speak. What was I to do? To scream would not have availed me in that attic, — and yet I wonder now I did not try to scream. I tore my hands away from him and sprang from my seat, he not seeking to restrain me, but still kneeling and gazing up at me with wild but penitent eyes.

"Open the door, sir, and let me go! That is the least return you can make for your rudeness," I said.

"No, no, no!" he cried with a wail of grief. "I have insulted my goddess. I have broken her heart. She will not speak to me. But look, look!" he said, darting again toward the canvas and throwing aside the drapery. "She is here! I have her here forever. No one can rob me of her now."

Fancy my emotions. It was a portrait of myself!

I shall never forget the tipsy cunning of Paul Barr's expression, as he watched the effect of his legerdemain. The portrait was excellent; it was, indeed, a masterpiece. I was sufficiently in my senses to appreciate that, though my absorbing thought was how to get out of the room. For some moments we each kept our pose, — I standing surveying the picture, and he with his eyes bent upon me, leaning against the easel which was in the pathway to the door.

Suddenly, and to my intense surprise, he pronounced my name, —

"Virginia!"

It was a whisper almost, and spoken as one might breathe the name of a saint.

"Virginia!"

Then with a low cry he stepped forward a pace or two and dropped on his knees again.

"I love you, I adore you. I have broken your heart, my angel, but it was love that forced me to it. Forgive me, and tell me if you can that there is hope, — a shadow is enough. Hope that I may some day press you to this bosom and call you mine, — mine for eternity! Virginia, hear me! — do not look so cold and cruel; you are a stone, while I am burning! I have loved you since the first moment I saw you. I wish my heart were dust for you to trample on, if it may not beat forever close to yours. With you as my bride I could conquer worlds. I could become an Angelo, a Rubens. Without you I shall die!"

He seized my hands again and covered them with kisses.

"Mr. Barr, Mr. Barr! I cannot listen to you further. Let me go, — you are mad."

"Yes, I am mad,— mad with love for you, sweet Virginia."

I tried to speak calmly, yet decisively, though from fear and pity I was trembling like a leaf. I told him that I could not grant what he asked. I loved him as a friend, as a brother almost, and would do anything to serve him but consent to become his wife. His studio was no place for such a conversation, I said. Let him come to my house, after he had thought it over. He would agree then that he had been carried away by the impulse of the moment, by the tension of his overstrained nerves, and that a marriage between us would be an absurdity. Were not our tastes and habits totally unlike?

Perhaps these were no words to address to an overwrought soul, mastered by passion. But, as I have said, I was terrified and bewildered. The strong desire I felt to treat him with all the gentleness and tender consideration I could muster, must have been to some extent neutralized by my anxiety to put an end to the interview. As I spoke, his eyes seemed to grow darker and to glow with fire, and the cunning, satyr-like expression I had noticed before to intensify.

"Pardon me," I said, "for the pain I cause you. My presence can only increase your suffering. I will leave you, and if you wish, we will talk of this to-morrow."

"To-morrow!" he answered; "there may be no to-morrow. It is still to-day! still to-day!" he repeated with a sort of chuckle. "I will live to-day, though I may die to-morrow. My goddess, my queen is here, and love — love — love!" With a bound he folded me in his huge arms and pressed my face against his lips three times in a mad embrace.

"Coward! wretch!" I screamed; but I was powerless as a babe.

He let me go.

"I will not hurt you, my own true love. A kiss can do no harm. Once more!" and he threw his arms wide open for a fresh embrace.

But another voice interrupted his purpose. "Coward! you shall not touch a hair of her head."

It was Mr. Spence who spoke; we had not noticed the door open. He strode forward and placed himself between me and the artist. On the threshold stood Miss Kingsley, and I felt the blood rush to my cheeks as our eyes met. I would gladly have given half my fortune to blot out the past few minutes.

"Is this the courtesy of Bohemia?" asked Mr. Spence, breaking the silence that followed. He was pale, and his lips were set, and there had never seemed to me so little difference in stature between him and Mr. Barr.

"It is love," was the answer. "The rapture of those kisses will be on my lips to my dying day." The artist began to troll the words of a mad song of his own composition I had heard before.

"Paul Barr, though we have long differed on many subjects, we have been friends. But after what I have heard and seen to-day, we must meet henceforth as strangers," said Mr. Spence, with a fire I had never known him display before.

"I adore her, and I am human. See there!" he pointed to the portrait, which hitherto had escaped their attention. "I would give even that for another kiss."

At the sight of the picture Mr. Spence gave a start, for the likeness was marvellous. As for Miss Kingsley, she whispered in my ear, —

"Did you sit for it, dear?"

"No, I did not," I answered.

"Detestable philosophy!" continued Mr. Spence, looking from the canvas to the artist. "There was the making of a man in you, — this portrait shows it. But it is too late. The brute is rampant, and genius is no more."

"She could have moulded me in her hands like clay," said Paul Barr. I could not help feeling touched by the despair in his voice.

"How distinctly piteous!" murmured Miss Kingsley.

"I have no more to say. You have heard my decision, Paul Barr."

Mr. Spence seemed greatly moved and excited. I could see him tremble. It was very bitter to me to feel that on my account friends of a lifetime were to be separated. The big artist pulled at his beard, and with another of his faun-like looks, exclaimed, —

"I understand. You want her for yourself. But you cannot rob me of those kisses, ha! ha! They shall lie in the grave with me, and I shall still smile."

Mr. Spence grew paler yet. He seemed about to speak, but controlling himself by an effort turned to leave the room, motioning us to precede him.

"How distinctly piteous!" repeated Miss Kingsley, as we went downstairs. "He acted shamefully, of course, and there is no excuse for his conduct. But though it is impossible to justify him, I can pity him, can't you? His nature is so impressionable; and when he is interested in anything there is no half way with him: he wants the whole or nothing. If you will excuse my saying so, several of us have been afraid of something of this sort. I wanted to warn you; but I said to myself, 'It may be Virginia really likes him,' so I decided not to speak. If I had done so, all this might have been prevented, for it was very evident to the rest of us that he was desperately in love with you. And by such a man, of course the very smallest marks of favor are construed as more significant than open encouragement would be by a less poetic temperament. I have no doubt the poor fellow wears over his heart every rose-bud you ever gave him, and knows by rote every word of sympathy you ever said to him. And then that portrait, — what volumes it tells of itself! Fancy that ardent soul toiling over the canvas to reproduce from memory your image (you tell me you did not sit to him), and when the masterpiece of his life was finished, inviting you to his studio (as I suppose he did), and then in a moment of deep and passionate love casting himself at your feet — and — and forgetting himself! Oh, Virginia, there is something exquisitely pathetic in the thought! But how fortunate too for you that we arrived when we did! In his sober senses Paul Barr would rather die than injure a hair of your head; but none of us, however self-reliant, is free from dread in the presence of a man who has been over-indulging in stimulants, even though sure of his affection. My poor dear, how you must have suffered! What will your Aunt Agnes say? It was only two days ago she said to me she hoped the affair was at an end. I told her then that one can never be sure of a thoroughly Bohemian nature; it is liable to burst into flame at the moment one least expects it. The result shows the correctness of my prediction. Poor Mr. Barr! what will become of him I wonder? I only hope he will not attempt his own life, — that would be worse than anything."

Neither Mr. Spence nor I had spoken as she rattled on in this manner, going down the long flights of stairs to the street. There was just enough of truth in her remarks to make my frame of mind still more wretched, and I could barely refrain from requesting her to keep still. Mr. Spence was evidently much disturbed by what had occurred. The expression of his face showed that he was under the influence of violent emotions. Once or twice, too, I saw him glance almost impatiently at Miss Kingsley, as if her prattle annoyed him. But she was so brimming over with volubility as to be blind to everything but the fancies she saw fit to evoke in regard to the scene she had just witnessed.

When, however, we reached a crossing of streets where her way separated from mine, Mr. Spence said, in a tone that for him was abrupt, "I shall see Miss Harlan home."

Miss Kingsley held my hand for a parting shot. "You must not think me unsympathetic, dear, because I feel sorry for poor Paul Barr. I knew him before you did, you know; and at one time we were quite as intimate, though in a different way. If you feel faint, as I should think you must after such a dreadful experience, why don't you stop at an apothecary's and get some salts? I always intend to carry salts with me; they are so convenient on an occasion of this sort. I do hope you will feel better to-morrow, dear. I shall call the first thing in the morning to inquire about you. Good-night."

For some minutes Mr. Spence and I remained silent. But now that Miss Kingsley was gone I felt an impulse to thank him, and to explain, so far as was possible, my presence at the studio.

"Believe me, Mr. Spence, I am very grateful to you for your aid," I began. "It was very inconsiderate and imprudent of me to go there alone; but he was so anxious for me to see the picture before any one else, that I was foolish enough to consider it allowable. I had no idea that it was a portrait of me, and none that he cared for me in the way it seems he does. I have tried to be kind to him, for I felt he was lonely, and might be saved from excesses by a sympathetic influence. But I see my mistake now. I ought to have known."

An indefinable wish that Mr. Spence should know the exact truth loosened my tongue.

"I understand — I understand perfectly," he said in an emotional tone. "It is I that am to blame. I might have prevented it," he added, as though speaking to himself.

Surprise prevented me from saying more, for I could not see how Mr. Spence was in any way responsible. Nor did he, on his part, continue the conversation. In five minutes we were at my door.

"Will you not come in, Mr. Spence?"

"No, not to-night." He paused an instant.

"At what hour are you likely to be at home and disengaged to-morrow?" he asked with suddenness.

"To-morrow? At almost any time. Shall we say four?"

Mr. Spence bowed by way of acquiesence. He seemed so stiff that I feared he was offended with me. But if so, why did he wish to come to-morrow?

"Before you go, you must let me thank you once more for having saved me from a very awkward predicament," I said, holding out my hand. "What should I have done if you had not arrived?" I shuddered involuntarily.

"Poor girl, how you must have suffered!" he exclaimed in a voice full of feeling. Then he turned abruptly and left me.

VI.

AS soon as I was safe at home, a terrible reaction followed. I went to bed prostrated physically, and sick at heart. True as it doubtless was that Paul Barr would never voluntarily have insulted me, I had deliberately exposed myself to the tipsy eccentricities of a man whose habits were not unknown. Might I not also have discovered, if I had been wholly candid with myself, that there was genuine feeling in the words of devotion he had so frequently whispered to me, and that under the extravagance of his behavior there lurked a vein of real sentiment? So much is apparent and stands out in another light when one looks back instead of forward! But this much was true at least, — I was disillusioned forever of the hope of successfully proselytizing Bohemia under the guise of sympathy. Mingled with the bitter tears of regret for the suffering of which I had been the cause were resolves that henceforth I would not sneer at conventionality and custom.

However much I might be devoted to thought and study, I would practise the ordinary precautions of my sex, and recognize the uses of matrons.

The next day was Christmas, and before I returned from church Miss Kingsley had called. There was a letter from Paul Barr awaiting me,— and such a letter! In it humiliation, despair, poetry, and passion were intermingled. Tears had blurred the pages, and I wept in turn as I read the pitiful sentences. He could not hope for pardon, he said, but he should never cease to love. He wished to die. What would be fame unless shared with the idol of his soul? Existence was for him henceforth a dreary waste; and yet his only fault had been that in the ecstasy of heaven-sent passion he had overleaped the bounds imposed by human pettiness.

As I read on, his burning words seemed almost intended as a defence. He had outraged my feelings, and for that he was to-day suffering exquisite torture, he said; but in the next paragraph he railed against the social prejudices of the age and the luke-warm character of contemporary love. In another century, he prophesied, the artificial barriers imposed by a narrow and fast-rotting civilization would be swept away by the mighty wave of passion which, pent up in the bosoms of strong men through a score of generations, was about to inundate the world. Under the impulse of this idea, the closing portions of his twelve-paged letter became a fierce tirade against the existing state of society; but the last sentence was so astonishing to me individually, that I blushed with the acuteness of my feelings. "Believing as I do," he wrote, "in the expansion and overflow of the human soul, I would fain have saved you from the cramped and bloodless nature to which you are about to ally yourself in preference to mine. He has robbed me of you, and thereby broken the last tie which held together our conflicting dispositions. With him you can never be supremely happy or supremely miserable,—which seems to me a lot so wretched that my heart, though heavy with the anguish of its own sorrow, is wrung more with pity than with pain."

His meaning was obvious, and I was still sitting with this strange epistle in my lap when Mr. Spence arrived. It would be affectation to say I was greatly surprised, when, after a few moments, he made to me a confession of his love. From his words of the previous evening, from a host of little indications which they had recalled to me, and finally from the jealous suspicions of the unhappy artist, I was not wholly unprepared for this result. There was nothing in the manner of his declaration that calls for mention. It was, as he said, a confession long deferred and struggled against, but he had been mastered at last by a power stronger than himself. He had come, he said, to make this acknowledgment of his feelings, no matter what might be the result; for there was something he must ask me to listen to, which it would be needful that I should know before he could dare to ask me to become his wife, or I should be able to answer.

I felt I knew what he was about to say, and was not mistaken. The question with most young people, he said, was how to find the means upon which to marry; but in his case those means were already provided, and a difficulty of a precisely opposite character stood between him and me. I must have perceived by this time his intense devotion to the system of philosophy of which he was the chief advocate. He had sacrificed everything in life to that one end, and he was prepared to do so so long as he was spared to labor. To practise in every way, so far as was possible, the principles he professed was the only escape, in his opinion, from that worst stigma of would-be-reformers, — hypocrisy. Among the leading obstacles, in his judgment, to a well-ordered life was the accumulation of property beyond enough to satisfy the common needs and comforts of life. He had taken the vow of approximate poverty, — not the extreme obligation of the clerical orders, but a limited, moderate view in accordance with the views just expressed. In seeking a partner to aid him with her support and sympathy in the great up-hill struggle to which he had consecrated his powers, he had wished to make choice of a woman with but small means, if any; but fate had willed otherwise. Once already — he said that he desired to conceal nothing — he had offered himself to a young lady of large property, for whom he felt a deep attachment. He had asked her, as he was about to ask me, to give herself to him in return for his love, without her fortune. With that she was free to do what she wished; it would be easy to dispose of it. After debate she refused him. This was six years ago; and until he saw me no thought of love had refreshed his heart. On that night at Miss Kingsley's, when he saw me for the first time and before he knew of my father's wealth, he loved me, he said, almost without knowing it; but from the moment of hearing the words that warned him of the barrier between us, he had striven to drive my image from his thoughts. Ever since, with all the might and resolution of which he was capable, he had struggled against his love, but in vain. He had tried to avoid my presence; he had resisted the temptation to become my teacher at the time I consulted him on the subject; and subsequently, when we were brought into constant contact at the rooms of the society, he had offended his own sense of politeness by the reserve of his behavior toward me. But, despite all this, he had felt the ground gradually slipping from beneath his feet. A chance look or smile nullified in an instant the self-denial of weeks. He had been many times already on the verge of an avowal. He had seen and heard from others of the intimacy between Mr. Barr and me, and been tortured by the pangs of jealousy. But the events of yesterday had made it impossible for him to remain silent any longer. He loved me with all the fervor of his heart, and it was vain for him to deny it.

He paused, but I remained silent. Spoken in his soft melodious voice his words seemed to soothe me, by way of contrast to the storm of passion I had listened to so recently. I did not try to think. I felt that he had not finished, and I wished to hear him to the end. Perhaps I was conscious, too, that it would be impossible for me to come to a decision on the spot.

One circumstance, he continued, had given him hope that I might feel ready to make the sacrifice he asked, provided that I returned his love, — and that was the earnest spirit of interest I had shown in the work he had undertaken. There was no one among his followers who seemed so completely zealous, and who had so unreservedly labored for the cause of Moderation, as I. If, then, my heart by chance were interested in the founder as well as in the system, it might seem no very serious matter to disclaim the wealth I should inherit from my father. It appeared to him that a nature like mine might find a higher and more entire happiness in the pursuit of ideal truth than in the enjoyment of an excess of money contrary to the whispers of a sensitive conscience. And if at the same time this renunciation of that which less enlightened souls esteemed as a chief good should be abetted by the sympathy of a companion soul, what bliss might not be in store for two lives so wedded to progress and to love!

Such was the substance of Mr. Spence's communication; and when he ceased, my feelings were still so doubtful that I sat looking into space as though to find counsel elsewhere than from my own heart. He had spoken,— deemed it only right to speak, he said,— before closing, of the criticism to which so unusual an act would expose me. I should be called eccentric, and doubtless by many crazy; and the terms of contempt and ridicule already cast at him would be visited, in equal degree, upon his wife. It was this idea of martyrdom, joined to the deep interest I had in the doctrines of Moderation, that now took possession of my fancy and made me incline to accede to his request. Not that I sought ostracism and abuse, — far from it; the very mention of these things oppressed me with dread. But there was to me an inspiring sense of nobility in the thought of a man giving up his life to the prosecution of a great truth indifferent to scoffs and sneers, that made the blood course more swiftly through my veins. If such a one could be made happier, and his power of usefulness increased by any act of mine, no sacrifice seemed too large. For what was I, or what was the value of anything I might do, compared with the progress of humanity as a whole? I could not give him love, perhaps, and the freshness of a young heart; but sympathy and encouragement and the co-operation of a mind deeply interested in the cause with which he was identified, might do much to make the struggle more easy and success speedier. Was I likely ever to meet with any one more congenial? What better use could I make of my life?

These thoughts came to me not only then, but afterwards when Mr. Spence had gone and I was left alone to make up my mind. I had told him that he must give me time; it was impossible for me to decide at the moment. What he had said was so bewildering, and the condition of any possible marriage between us of so serious a character, that I was at a loss for an answer. But I warned him not to feel too much encouragement because I did not give him an immediate reply; the chances were more than likely that upon reflection I should feel what he asked to be impossible. "I respect you thoroughly, Mr. Spence, and I am much interested in your work; but I do not think I should ever love you as you would wish. I feel quite sure of it; but if you are disposed to let me think it over instead of giving you at once an unfavorable reply, I am willing to do so."

Both my aunts dined with us, it being Christmas day, and directly upon her arrival Aunt Helen remarked upon my paleness. It was an unusually silent meal for a Christmas gathering. My father, as I remembered later, seemed absorbed and dull. Aunt Agnes had shown me by a glance that the events of the previous day were not unknown to her. She sat glum and statuesque; but I did not attempt either to brave or to mollify her displeasure, for I knew that compared with the secret in my possession, the wretched affair with Paul Barr would seem to her a mere trifle. I wondered, however, what she would think of such a match. How surprised she would be, and how disappointed probably in Mr. Spence! — for I had little question that she regarded him as too much engrossed in his work ever to think of marriage. Indeed, she had said as much to me when I spoke of Miss Kingsley in that connection. Poor Miss Kingsley! it would be a cruel, bitter blow to her. I believed her to be in love with Mr. Spence, so far as it was possible for any woman to be interested in a man who had not made her an offer; and with the pardonable sense of triumph I experienced was mingled some pity. She was the first to detect the infatuation I had awakened in him, but his subsequent reserve had almost lulled her jealousy to sleep. I knew in advance what Aunt Helen would think. She would regard my conduct as little short of madness, and all sympathy between us would be at an end forever.

But it was my father's opinion on the subject that I most feared to face. I could not doubt what his verdict would be. It was the ambition of his later life to see me use well the fortune he had accumulated. By the marriage I was contemplating I should disappoint these expectations, for I could not suppose he would regard as a good use of the money a disclaimer of the fortune he wished to leave me. It was really between him and Mr. Spence that I must decide.

This was what presented itself to me clearly, as my father and I sat together in the library after my aunts had gone. It was past midnight, and yet neither of us had thought apparently of going to bed. He was smoking, and like myself busy with his own reflections. It seemed to me that he looked tired and worn. I had observed it several times of late. Was I certain that I was right in the choice I was tempted to make? But if I did not marry Mr. Spence, what was the prospect before me? What did my father wish me to do with his money?

As though he understood my silent question, he turned to me suddenly and said, —

"As you may remember, Virginia, I told you — it must be more than two years ago, now — that I was a very rich man. The same is true to-day, though, owing to the severe depression from which all classes of property have suffered during that period, I am no longer as wealthy as I was. Indeed, it has been only by unflagging attention and care that I have been able to avoid very serious losses. But let that pass. Confidence is restored, and the worst is over. My affairs are in a shape now where further depreciation is well-nigh impossible, and you will have all the money that you can possibly need when I am gone."

He paused a moment, and I hastened to express my concern that he had been worried.

"That is all done with now, I hope. I only mentioned it in order that you should know what you have to expect,—and because I have been making up my accounts for the first of the year. No one can tell what another year may bring forth. I am not so strong as I was, I think."

He spoke without emotion; but there was something in his tone that prompted me to go to him, and kneeling by his side to take his hand in mine.

"Are you not well, father?"

"Oh, yes. But when a man has worked hard all his days and gets to be sixty-five years old, the machine does not run so smoothly as it used. That is all. Some day it will stop all of a sudden, just as it did in my father's case. He was worn out when he died; and that is what I shall be. In this country, we most of us have only time to get together our millions and die." He spoke with a smile, and gently stroked my hair. "But we expect our children to make a good use of the leisure we have won for them. You begin where I leave off, Virginia. I had hoped to be able to see a great deal of you during the last few years, but just at the moment when I was about to lay aside the harness came the period of depression. It is very difficult, in this country, for parents to know their children intimately. Neither party has time for the operation. You have your interests, as well as I; and what is more, I scarcely know what they are. I am not complaining; I am merely stating facts. If my life is spared a few years longer, we will try to change all that. Before I die I should like to see you happily married to some one who is worthy of you. Nothing ever gave me so much pain as to see you suffer at the time that fellow deceived you, — nothing at least except the thought of your becoming his wife. But that is past, thank Heaven! and I think I am right in saying that you have forgotten him long since."

He talked in a half soliloquizing fashion, in short, deliberate sentences, and looked up to me as he finished, for a confirmation of his opinion.

"A woman never forgets, father. But I am very glad you saved me from marrying him."

"Yes, yes, it would have been madness," he replied eagerly. "I could not have endured the thought of that good-for-nothing squandering my property. I should never have relented, and I should have been in my grave before this. But let by-gones be by-gones. To-day you are older and wiser, and I have confidence that you will keep the credit of our name untarnished. It has taken three generations of honest men to accumulate the fortune you will inherit," he added proudly.

"But what do you wish me to do with it, father?"

"That is for you to decide when I am gone. I could tell you how to make money, and how to keep it, perhaps; but how to spend it wisely requires a different sort of talent than I possess. I have told you, from the first, that it was to be your life-work. Busy as I have been, I have tried to place the means of understanding the commercial value of money in your way, so that you might not be wholly ignorant when the time came to act."

"And it would be a bitter disappointment to you, then, if I were to give it all up?"

"Give it up?" he glanced at me with a comical expression, as though I had said something preposterous. "You couldn't give it up if you wanted to. It will come to you by my will. I shall leave it all in your hands."

For a few moments I did not reply. Then I turned to him and said: —

"You were speaking just now of wishing to see me happily married, and you referred to Mr. Dale."

"Well?"

"Don't be concerned, father. It is not of him I wish to speak, except to say that though I have been very grateful he is not my husband, I do not believe I shall ever care for anybody else in the same way. But I have had, this very day, an offer of marriage from a man who is in every sense worthy of me. Indeed, I am not worthy of him."

"Of whom are you speaking?"

"Of Mr. Spence, father."

"Spence? I do not recall the name."

"You have met him only once, I think. He came to the house one afternoon, about a year ago, with that Mr. Barr who dines here sometimes."

"Oh!"

I cannot give a precise idea of that ejaculation. It was a strange mixture of pleasantry and consternation.

"He is by profession a poet, — and a philosopher. His writings are highly thought of among literary people, and he is an intimate friend of Aunt Agnes," I said quietly.

"What answer did you give him?" asked my father presently, with a weary air. He leaned his head on his hand, and listened intently and anxiously.

"I told him I would think the matter over," I replied.

"He is not the husband I would have chosen for you, Virginia," he said, after a silence. "But you must suit yourself. Now that you recall him to me, I know who this Mr. Spence is. I have seen his name in the newspapers, and a few weeks ago I remember he delivered a lecture before the Thursday Evening Club. It was a visionary, unpractical address, I thought. Several members spoke to me of it as such. But there were one or two enthusiasts — as there are everywhere — who extolled it as a marvel of originality and cleverness. Are you sure of his habits?"

"His habits ought to be good, for he is the advocate of the theory of Moderation. It is to that he devotes the greater part of his time. Yes, father, I am sure of them."

"I remember now, — Moderation. That was what he talked about. He is one of your so-called reformers. He gets hold of an idea and tries to fit the world to it. And you say you wish to marry him, Virginia?"

"I have not said so. I don't know."

"If you take my advice, you will not. I know nothing further of him than you have told me. The better philosopher a man is, the worse husband he is likely to make. Has he anything to live upon?"

"Yes; enough to support us comfortably, I believe. In fact, he does not wish me to take any money from you."

"That shows him a more independent minded fellow than I supposed. Humph! One literary woman in the family ought to be enough. Still, the great thing is that you should be suited. We are not all cut after the same pattern, and if you have a fancy for a husband of that type, I shall not stand in the way. I interfered once, but that was a very different matter. Satisfy me that there is nothing objectionable against this Mr. Spence, and if you wish to marry him I shall not offer serious opposition. It is all nonsense about your not being able to care for anybody. If you like a man well enough to become his wife, the rest will follow. I should be glad to see you married."

"I like Mr. Spence very much; but it is his theory of Moderation that interests me even more than himself," I answered, uncertain how to lead up to the condition of our marriage, which I knew now would irritate my father greatly. He had received the news of Mr. Spence's offer much more favorably than I expected. It was evident he wished me to marry some one.

"As you have said, father, I have interests of my own of which you do not know. I have given five hours almost every day during the past year to the study of the principles of this philosophy. I have found my field of usefulness there, it seems to me. By continuing this work and becoming the wife of Mr. Spence, I feel that I shall be doing more good in the world than I could in any other way. If you ask me if I love Mr. Spence, candor compels me to say that I do not. If you ask if I am particularly happy at the prospect of marrying him, I must say that I am not. But it seems to me the best chance that is likely to offer. I respect him thoroughly, and, as you say, the rest may follow. A life devoted to a noble theory is better suited to my tastes and capacities than the control of a large fortune."

"You are a little morbid, Virginia," he interrupted. "My original impression is confirmed. This is no match for you. I warn you against the danger of becoming addicted to *fads* and *isms*. Your Aunt Agnes has made herself ridiculous and alienated all her friends by just such a course. I have not a word to say against a thorough education, as you must well know; but when a woman begins to talk about devoting her life to the principles of philosophy, 'Look out!' say I. It is not natural. She needs a new bonnet, and a few balls and parties. But even supposing you marry this Socrates and become as learned as he, how is that inconsistent with taking care of your fortune?"

"I thought I told you, father," I said.

"Told me what?"

"That Mr. Spence objected to my fortune."

"Objected, did he? How is he to help himself? Besides, the money is mine until I am dead. If he is so infernally proud, he need n't touch any of it until then. I fancy he might get tired of waiting."

"You don't understand, father. Mr. Spence wants me to agree never to touch any of it. He does n't think it right for people to keep more than a certain amount, just enough to provide for their actual needs. It is one of the principles he believes in. It is a part of his system."

"Principles! System! Is the girl crazy?"

"It is opposed to all your ideas, I know," I exclaimed earnestly, determined now that I had entered on the matter to dispute it with vigor. "But are you sure that you are in the right?

What is the use of so much money to a woman? You want me to make the most of the fortune it has taken you all your life to get together. Is it not possible that in renouncing it I should be doing that? New ideas have to encounter opposition, but they are not all to be presumed unsound on that account. There may be more sense in those of Mr. Spence than you suppose. By setting this example of moderation, I may be able to give an impetus to truth that will be of real service to mankind. Besides, women are different from men, father. They find more comfort and happiness in devotion to something like this than in the practical details of life. I have had some experience. I have seen society, and know the weariness of a merely social existence. As I have already told you, I believe I should be more content with Mr. Spence than with any one else. I need sympathy and an interest. I *am* morbid, perhaps; but there is every chance of my becoming more so unless you let me have my way in this matter. Leave your money to some deserving charity or college, father, and let me marry Mr. Spence."

"Deserving charity or college! That from the lips of my own daughter! I have wanted to interrupt you a dozen times to tell you how foolish and senseless is the rubbish you were talking. And now that I have heard you to the end, I am speechless. You are crazy! I repeat it, crazy! You are fit only for a convent or a lunatic asylum. I had better find another heir."

He covered his face with his hands, and I could see his whole form tremble.

"Father," I cried, "if I were only sure that you are not mistaken!"

We sat without another word being spoken for many minutes. At last he lay back in his chair with the weary air intensified which I had noticed when I told him of Mr. Spence's offer, and said in a tone in harmony with that, —

"You have been brought up, Virginia, like all American girls, to have your own way. I have given you every indulgence and liberty. Your smallest wish has been regarded. If I could wipe out the past and begin anew, I feel that I should act very differently. I should wield a rod of iron, and teach my own flesh and blood to obey by saying, 'Do this!' and 'You shall not do that!' The result could be no worse than it has been under the other system. Is the judgment of the new generation so infallible," he continued, "that it can afford to dispense with obedience and filial respect altogether? You have had one lesson already, Virginia, but you have failed to profit by it. When that fortune-hunting, idle dandy was whispering his pretty speeches in your ear, was it your own good sense that saved you from a miserable alliance? No; if I had not for once in my life stepped in and said, 'You do this thing at your own peril,' and proved to you the paltry soul of the fellow, what would you be to-day? Broken-hearted and old before your time. But that was when you were almost a child, and without experience. I was made very unhappy, but I said to myself, 'She will grow wiser as she grows older.' And I thought you had. In the multitude of my business cares I have merely had time to observe you in a general way. But I supposed the serious and absorbed air which your face has worn came from the interest of your studies, and that those studies were fitting you for the work I had planned for you. I wish now that you had never touched a book in your life. Better in my opinion to be the careless butterfly of society than the fanatic. I never expected to live to see my only child so blind to common-sense as to wish to follow such a monstrous theory as you have described. Money! Why, it is the power and possibility of the world. But what good are words? If you cannot see the folly and unsoundness of it at a glance, it is useless for me to talk. Go your own ways. Marry whom you like. Not a dollar of my money —"

He stopped as he realized the futility of his threat, and covered his face again with his hands.

Looking back over many years, it seems to me at times incredible that I should have held out so long against such entreaty and distress; but it is to be said on the other hand that my whole future happiness was involved in the decision of the question. My natural obstinacy had deepened as I listened to his words, and had tended to counteract the affection and pity I felt for him.

"If I were only sure that you are right!" I repeated. "What you say about my education is perfectly true. I *have* been brought up to have my own way, but also, father, to have no counsel but my own. If so much freedom has been given me, was it not with the idea of teaching me to make up my own mind about things? And if I have made up my mind, and I feel my conscience urge me to take a step which involves my happiness for the rest of my life, why is it unfilial of me to follow my own judgment? I have been alone, and thrown upon my own responsibility, ever since I was a child. I am not complaining. I have had no mother; you have been busy down-town, and my aunts never agree in their advice. I have tried to think for myself. I have chosen an interest in life to which I am ready to devote my best energies, and in order to do so more completely should, if you did not forbid, marry a man who is in every way my superior, and whom I thoroughly respect. I am willing to give this all up to please you. But I do not mean, father, that I think you are in the right. I am no longer the child I was when I wished to disobey you before. Then I refused to yield, until you convinced me that I was wrong. To-day I am prepared to sacrifice my own wishes for your sake, but I remain unconvinced. I will write to Mr. Spence to-night, and tell him that I cannot be his wife. I will resign my position as secretary of his Society, and give up what you call *fads* and *isms*. Only I shall expect for the future, father, that you will tell me precisely what you wish me to do, and let me do it. You must not deprive me of my liberty of choice, and then treat me just as if I were free. Do with me what you will. Marry me to whom you please. I will obey,— implicitly, unhesitatingly. Only take away from me the responsibility once and for all. I am weary of it."

I had spoken with anger and excitement. My nerves were all unstrung by the events of the past two days; and as I finished, my tears burst forth. I wept with passionate sobs. My father made no effort to comfort me. He sat with his chin resting on his breast, weary and sad.

"I did not mean to be disrespectful," I murmured at last. "I am willing to do all that you desire."

"You have said that you do not love this man, Virginia."

"I love him as much as I shall ever love any one else," I answered.

"I accept your sacrifice, my child. Some day you will thank me. But write to-night. I shall sleep better if I feel that it is done. Promise me," he added, looking at me with a strange eagerness that was pathetic, and made the tears return to my eyes, but this time out of tenderness,— " promise me that whatever happens, you will accept the trust I am going to leave you."

I ran to his side, and kneeling, raised my eyes to his,—"Forgive me, father! I promise faithfully."

Only a few words more need to be said concerning this phase of my life. That night I wrote to Mr. Spence. Gratitude and friendship will not make up for the absence of love, but whatever there can be of consolation in these substitutes I sent to him. Why was it that as I penned the lines which were to disappoint his hopes, I was vaguely conscious that my interest in his theories was already less? So difficult is it in life to determine precisely how far our beliefs are decided by our associations! But it is not to be supposed that because I admit this after the lapse of years, the consciousness of which I speak was at that time more than a secret one, which I shrank from confessing even to myself. Genuine were the tears I shed in private for many days. My life seemed to me a blank, and I had lost the motive of action. For allowing my father to be right, and the principles advocated by Mr. Spence to be monstrous and absurd, I had been too intimately connected with the system not to feel a great void in my existence at severing my relations with it. What was to take its place?

I had to undergo, moreover, one or two disagreeable interviews with my Aunt Agnes before the matter was finally settled. In the intensity of his disappointment, Mr. Spence applied to her and asked her to endeavor to alter my resolution. She sent for me, and though she did not disguise her surprise that her favorite should wish to marry at all, she was unequivocal in the expression of her opinion that I should never get such another chance. As I remained obdurate, she accused me of a deliberate attempt to trifle with his affections. I had already ruined the life of one man of genius, she said, who though a wanderer from the right path might reasonably have become a noble worker but for my influence; and now I was about to blight the happiness of one whose equal was to be found only a few times in a century. She even went to my father, and represented to him the folly I would commit in refusing such an offer. I was not present at the interview; but Aunt Agnes, as she came out of the library into the room where I was sitting, looked angry and severe.

"Money, money, money! That is all your father thinks of from morning until night. It is wearing on him too. It is killing him by inches."

"You are right, Aunt Agnes; he needs rest; he looks tired out," I said, ignoring the first part of her speech.

"It is his own fault. And now he wants to educate you in the same school. Lucretia Kingsley is correct, — oil and water are more fit to be mated than you and Mr. Spence. You have broken her heart, too, by your wanton conduct, Virginia. Her sympathy for Mr. Spence is very affecting."

"Pooh!" I answered, angered by her indifference regarding my father; "she is crazy to marry him herself. That is all the matter with her."

This was the last effort Aunt Agnes made to alter my resolution, but she saw fit to tell Aunt Helen of my escapade at Mr. Barr's studio, who came to me in horror. Her predictions were about to be realized, she said. Notwithstanding all her warnings, my name was associated with a vulgar adventurer. "A handsome wretch as I remember him," she added, "but — even on your aunt's admission, who is none too nice in her estimate of people — unprincipled, and with low agrarian tastes."

A fortnight after my dismissal of Mr. Spence, a misfortune befell me that banished all thoughts save those of grief. My father was seized with a sudden illness, and died within a few hours. The doctors said the cause of his death was disease of the heart, and that he had been aware of the existence of the disorder for some time. It was many days before I thought again of what I was told after the funeral, — that I was left by my father's will sole heiress to four million dollars.

BOOK III.

(UN)COMMON SENSE.

I.

MY first impulse was to become a woman of business, and assume the entire control of my inheritance. Excepting a few charitable bequests and some trifling legacies, everything was left to me. I was even made executrix; but my father had indicated in a separate paper that in regard to matters out of my knowledge I could safely consult his own legal adviser, Horatio Chelm.

Mr. Chelm was the conventional idea of a successful lawyer, — withered, non-committal, and a little fusty; but technicalities had failed to harden his heart or obscure his good sense. He had a sunny smile, which refreshed my sad spirit when I called upon him shortly after the funeral to inform him of my purpose, and made me feel that I could confide in him.

"What, my dear young lady! take entire charge of four million dollars? I admire your business ambition, but I must tell you that such a task is impossible, if you wish to have leisure for anything else. No, no! your father could not have meant that. I knew him well, and he was the last man to have wished to make you a slave to your good fortune. With an income of nearly two hundred thousand dollars you can afford to leave to some one else the anxiety and drudgery attendant on the care of your property. Your father wished you to enjoy his money and use it well. He has told me so himself. He was very fond and very proud of you, Miss Harlan."

"But he was very anxious to have me understand business matters, Mr. Chelm," I replied.

"And he was quite right, too. Don't think for a moment I am dissuading you from undertaking a general supervision of your property and trying to know all about it. It is your duty under the circumstances, I fully agree. But it would never do to have you spending the best years of your life cooped up in an office cutting off coupons and worrying over investments. Not, to be sure, that there is much to be done at present, for I never saw a cleaner list of securities than yours; but you have no idea of the amount of watchfulness required to keep an estate like this unimpaired. A family of children are nothing to it, ha! ha! No, Miss Harlan, I tell you what we will do; you shall have a little office adjoining mine, where you can spend one day in every week transacting what is necessary in regard to your property. Everything shall be in your name, and nothing done without your full understanding and consent. I will be at hand to be plied with questions, and you shall become as wise in finance as Necker himself. But I pray you to devote the six remaining days to other things, and leave to us dry, matter-of-fact lawyers the details of your business. I have a great many millions under my control, and the percentage which I should derive from the care of yours is a matter of indifference to me; but I am very much concerned that you should not make the fatal mistake of becoming a mere feminine trustee."

I yielded to persuasion; and in accordance with his promise a little room adjoining his own private office was allotted to me, and every Monday morning I drove down-town and spent the day in poring over the ledgers and deeds and reports, and in taking a general scrutiny of my affairs. At first it was all very confusing, but by degrees order was reduced out of chaos to my understanding, and I learned to take a keen interest in the points submitted to me for my decision. At first I felt some humiliation in perceiving that my opinion was consulted merely from form and courtesy, — or, more roughly, because the law required it. I was forced to laugh and shake my head and acknowledge that I was not capable of judging. I had hoped that I knew enough to be of service sometimes, and the consciousness of my ignorance spurred me to determined exertions to overcome the deficiency. Contrary to our compact, I read and studied at home books relating to financial and economical matters; I concealed railway reports in my muff, and tried various artifices to acquire knowledge unbeknown to Mr. Chelm. But it was chiefly to his kindness and unwearying attention that I owed the proficiency I gradually acquired; and I think it was as genuine a pleasure to him as to me, when at last I was able, with a moderate degree of confidence, to choose for myself between two lines of conduct. I often asked myself what I should have done had I attempted to act alone from the start.

But it was not long before another interest incident to and growing out of this began to occupy my thoughts and time. The bulk of my daily mail was increased by subscription lists and circulars soliciting my assistance to every kind of charity and enterprise. People whom I had never seen, came to the house to ask aid for struggling talent. I was importuned with begging letters from victims to all sorts of distress. Zealous philanthropists wrote that they had taken the liberty of putting down my name as a member of their societies, and that the annual assessment was now due and payable. Here again I had recourse to the counsel of Mr. Chelm, whose experience, as I have hinted, radiated beyond the limits of his lucrative practice, and who was not only liberal toward the poor, but familiar with their needs. From him I obtained a variety of hints and suggestions that enabled me to give my money and time intelligently, and also to refuse them without remorse. I was very glad of this new duty, which easily became a great pleasure despite my occasional disgust at the impertinence of some applicants when it was discovered that I was ready to subscribe freely. I was not however satisfied with the easy work of giving, but soon passed from the passive act of signing cheques to active work among the needy. I studied the theories of tenement houses and hygiene, and became a leading spirit in several charitable organizations.

I renewed also my old habit of reading, and no longer confined myself to the philosophic and dry subjects pursued under Mr. Fleisch. But I was conscious that the zest which I felt in renewing a wider range of study was due to the fact of my having acquired from his instruction a degree of industry and a power to appreciate that I had not previously possessed. At the suggestion of Mr. Chelm, whom I allured to chat with me regarding outside subjects when my business was finished, I read with regularity the leading newspapers and magazines. A familiarity with the former he declared to be indispensable to a knowledge of current affairs, and also that much of the freshest and most valuable thought of the day was first made public through the medium of periodicals. This practice received likewise the approval of Aunt Helen, who assured me that she always felt lost for the day if she had not looked at the Deaths and Marriages.

One of my first steps had been to ask Aunt Helen to come and live with me; to which she finally consented, though the consequent necessity of disestablishing her cosey little parlor, upon the embellishment of which she had spent the overflow of her income for years, cost her many a pang. But she was a far-seeing woman, and had I dare say, while accepting my offer, a delightful vision of helping me to live up to the duties of my position. I can only say that she soon began to impress the importance of this upon me by hints more or less palpable; and it was not long before she was to all intents and purposes the real house-keeper. It was still, to be sure, I that ordered the dinners and engaged the servants, but even in these minor details I was alive to her suggestions; while in the matter of the general direction of what went on, her wishes were supreme. At first I was too sad to be other than indifferent; and later it was a relief to me to have taken off my shoulders the bother of many things which I felt instinctively ought to be done. I could trust Aunt Helen's taste; and so she had my tacit permission to follow out her own inclinations in the way of change and improvements. Under her supervision the house was almost entirely refurnished and adorned with the most exquisite specimens of upholstery and bric-à-brac obtainable. So too, as time went on, she increased the number and raised the standard of the domestics, and persuaded me to buy a variety of horses and equipages. It was she who kept the grooms up to the mark regarding the proper degree of polish for the harnesses, and she spent many days in the selection of an artistic design for the crest to be emblazoned upon them. So far as was possible she represented that all these things were done at my desire and out of her sheer good nature. When I drove with her from shop to shop, as I often did to save myself from depressing thoughts, she invariably made me pass a formal approval upon whatever charmed her eye. If this innocent self-deceit gave her pleasure, it did not seem to me worth while to protest.

And so by the time I left off my mourning, there was little left to be done to make my establishment one of the most elegant in the city. Aunt Helen now turned her attention to my clothes. The costumes which I suffered her to select were marvels of Parisian art and New York adaptiveness. She sought too, by frequent allusions to my increased personal beauty, to arouse my vanity and induce me to throw off the pall of soberness that had settled upon my spirit. When this failed, she had recourse to an opposite policy, and repeated to me the remarks she overheard in coming out of church and elsewhere concerning me. Many of my acquaintances, she said, were of the opinion that I was eccentric and partial to "advanced" ideas. Another story current was that I had been compelled by my father on his death-bed, on pain of disinheritance, to dismiss a young artist to whom I was passionately attached. There was the same grain of truth to a bushel of error in the remaining conjectures; but Aunt Helen assured me that every one agreed I was peculiar, and deemed it unfortunate that a young lady possessed of such signal advantages should be different from all the rest of the world. Even I, unobservant as I was at this time, was made aware by the curious glances directed at me as I descended from my carriage, that to a certain extent an heiress belongs to the public.

Continual dropping, however, will wear away the hardest stone, and Aunt Helen was not one to weary in what she considered well-doing. When nearly three years had elapsed after my father's death, I yielded to her urgency and consented to inaugurate my return to society by giving a large ball. The idea came to me one night when I was feeling depressed and discouraged over my failure to obtain more than a passive sort of happiness in my present occupations. There were so many philanthropists, I thought. I had even begun to feel that the poor were extremely well provided for, and that in some respects they were really rather better off than

I was. For despite my studies and my hours with Mr. Chelm, and the society meetings which I attended, I was conscious at heart of being lonely. My ideas too had received certain impressions regarding the people who composed society that were quite foreign to those which had given me an aversion to it. Since my accession to an enormous fortune my attention had naturally been directed to the conduct of people situated similarly to myself. At first I was shocked and made morbid by the whirl of selfish pleasure and dissipation that seemed to characterize the lives of this class. But when I came to look a little deeper, I was surprised to find how many people among the rich whom I had judged to be simply frivolous and indifferent were in reality earnest workers in the various fields of philanthropy, science, or art, for the most part carrying on their investigations unobserved. Among them were a number of my old acquaintances with whom at the charitable and other gatherings where we met I had resumed the associations of four years ago; and I was struck by the serious spirit that now seemed to determine their actions. It was clear to me that earnest-minded people existed among the very wealthy no less than among those less fortunately circumstanced; and as this grew more apparent, I began to catch a glimpse of what my father had meant in speaking of wealth as the power and possibility of the world. Was it not essential to leisure; and leisure to refinement and culture? And where necessity ceased to control action, ought there not to be a greater chance for excellence and progress?

These growing impressions served to temper the almost morbid tendency of my thoughts to the extent that I have indicated. We gave a grand ball, and under the stimulus of the cordial welcome given me I became the gayest of the gay, and surprised not only my old acquaintances but myself by the vivacity and desire to please of which I proved capable. Without undue confidence, I can say that I achieved a triumph, and put to rout the various uncomplimentary conjectures that the world had hazarded in regard to me. Society opened its arms to me as a returning prodigal, and my revulsion of feeling was all the more spontaneous from the fact, that, if some of my former acquaintances were as frivolous as ever, they had learned to conceal their emptiness by an adaptability which made them agreeable companions. There was a keen satisfaction, too, in the consciousness which became mine, as I went from house to house during the following weeks, that I excelled the most of them in the power to make myself agreeable. The reading and study of the past few years enabled me to shine as a conversationalist, and in my present regenerated mood I had, on the other hand, no temptation to play the pedant or moralist. I tried to be amusing and to appear clever; and I was pleased to read a favorable verdict upon my effort in the attentions of men as a rule unsusceptible, and in the amazed countenance of Aunt Helen.

Her satisfaction at the course of events was not disguised; but she was diplomatic enough, in her conversations with me, not to take to herself the glory of the evolution. She contented herself by way of recrimination in such expressions as — "To think, Virginia, how near you came to throwing yourself away!" and, "It takes a great load off my mind to see you yourself once again." But after the first few entertainments at which we were present together, I often caught her looking at me with a sort of wonder, as though she could scarcely believe that the brilliant young person whose reappearance in the social world was the sensation of a successful season could really be her niece.

One evening as we were sitting after our return from an especially pleasant dinner-party, Aunt Helen surveyed me contentedly through her eye-glass, and said: —

"I have never seen you look or appear better in your life than you did to-night, my dear. Your dress set to perfection, and you were very agreeable."

I dropped a little curtsy in return.

"Yes," she continued, "I will not disguise that there was a time about a year ago when I felt very anxious in regard to you. Eccentricity, as I have often told you before, is all very well when one has nothing to lose and everything to gain by it. I can understand how a young person with no antecedents or opportunities for getting on in society might secure a temporary advantage by making herself an object of remark. But in your case it has always seemed to me wholly inexplicable. Every one knows who you are and all about you, already. However, all is well that ends well, and it is an unspeakable relief to me that you have come to your senses at last."

"Don't crow, Aunt Helen, until you are out of the woods. I may be merely a meteor that will vanish some day as quickly as I appeared, and leave you all in the dark."

"You are your own mistress, of course. If I take any credit to myself for what you are to-day, Virginia, it is because I have never interfered with anything you chose to do. I have expressed my opinion of course when I thought you were making mistakes, but I have stopped short at that. Others in the same position might have behaved differently; but it is not my way. I said to myself, 'If her own good sense does not teach her, nothing will.' So, too, now that you have justified my confidence in you, I have no temptation to act otherwise. You will do what you prefer, of course. But naturally I have my own ideas as to what is desirable for you."

"You have been very good to me always," I replied, smiling at this bland assumption of tact; "and I always like to hear what you have to say."

"Well, dear, it seems to me that with a very little trouble you can have the most attractive house in town. One hears it so often said that we have nothing to correspond to what the French call *salons*, — those delightful entertainments one reads about, where every one is either clever or distinguished. Of course every one is not really clever, but made to appear so,— the whole secret lying in the power of some charming and talented woman to select and combine harmoniously: even the most stupid people (if it is necessary to invite them) are made to say amusing things. You know of course what I mean. It has been tried here, but rarely with success. It requires both brains and personal attractions, and our women who possess one are too apt to imagine they have the other also. But it has occurred to me, several times lately, that you are just the person to attempt it. I may say without flattery, dear, that you are considered very handsome, and people have an impression that you are clever, — which is better even than really being so, and I do not mean to say that you are not, for I think you are. You have had an excellent education, and have a taste for books, and all that sort of thing. The fact that you have been known to be peculiar would rather add to your chances of success than otherwise, for it would throw a little air of mystery about you. Then you have a beautiful house and the means to entertain elegantly; and last, but not least, you have an assured position. The trouble is so apt to be, that those who attempt anything of the sort are not known. All the talent in the world will not be able to constitute a *salon* unless one possesses, and is intimate with others who possess, that indescribable something which every one understands, but which it is difficult to put into words. Yes, Virginia, you have a great opportunity before you, if only you choose to take advantage of it."

Curiously enough, this view of Aunt Helen was quite similar to certain ideas which I myself had been revolving since my return to conventional habits. I foresaw that my interest in balls and parties merely as such was sure to wane before long, and that if I wished to obtain continued diversion from society it must be by force of some such programme as that which she had suggested. In short, I felt that the tone and standard of social life might be raised if one set about it in the right way. As Aunt Helen said, there were really no reasons why my house should not become a centre of elegance and refinement, which, however far distant from the conception of a *salon*, might give pleasure of a legitimate sort to a large number of people.

So much did this scheme grow upon me, that by another winter I was busy in putting it into execution. Thanks to the past energy of Aunt Helen, my house was already very nearly up to the mark as a model of luxury and taste. I gave a series of entertainments which I sought to make as distinguished and agreeable as possible. Upon a foundation of the most fastidious and well-bred of my acquaintances I cast a sprinkling of clever men who commonly found parties a bore, original but outlandish women, representatives of every sort of talent, local and visiting celebrities, and every desirable stranger in town. They all would be glad to come for once, I knew. The vital point was to induce them to come again. To effect this, I left no stone unturned and begrudged no expenditure. I found it somewhat up-hill work at first, but none the less were my efforts crowned with success in the end. My house grew to be the favorite resort alike of the fashionable and the cultivated; and to keep it so created an interest in my life which relieved the sombreness of my other occupations.

In the pursuance of this object I gave free scope to a taste which I had been educating in a quiet way ever since my youth,— that of collecting pictures. I had a room in the house admirably adapted for the purpose fitted up as a gallery, and in a short time had got together the nucleus of a valuable display of masterpieces. By degrees it came to be known that this was the case, and I found pleasure in allowing the public to see them on certain days.

One day I was puzzled by the arrival of a picture carefully boxed up and addressed to me, which on opening I discovered to be the portrait of me which Paul Barr had painted. In selecting material for my entertainments I had naturally thought of him among the first, but inquiry failed to discover his whereabouts. He had left town a few days subsequent to the harassing scene between us, and there were no traces of him beyond the direction on the door of his studio that all communications intrusted to the janitor of the building would ultimately reach him. To this address I sent several notes of invitation, hoping perhaps to catch him on the wing or lure him from retirement. But at the time the portrait arrived I had ceased to make further attempts. There was no note or card accompanying it, but the bold superscription left no doubt in my mind as to the donor. A few weeks later I was astonished and delighted at one of my receptions to see the artist-poet's massive figure towering above the other guests, and an instant later we had exchanged the most cordial of hand-shakings, attended on his part as ever by profuse gesture and compliment, and on mine by genuine good-will, which it was easy to see he reciprocated. He looked little changed, unless it were that he was handsomer and more extraordinary than formerly, and his presence caused much lively speculation as to the new celebrity I had unearthed. He had been abroad, studying and travelling, — and trying to forget, he added. The last he had found impossible, he said; but though he sighed as he spoke, I knew that his wound was healed. He was to resume his work at once; had brought back a host of ideas he was eager to put into execution, and was what he called "under the mastery of the twin demi-gods — necessity and aspiration."

Later I thanked him for his picture, which I told him, as was notably the case, artistic circles were raving over. Indeed, when I let it be known that the handsome stranger was no other than Paul Barr, whose genius was already celebrated, he received an ovation. Nor was it exhausted at my house. He was instantly taken up by the critics and by fashionable folk alike, to such an extent that I became apprehensive lest so much attention would detract from the merit of his new work. But though I feared from what was whispered concerning him that his temperament and habits were still mercurial, he had evidently studied to some purpose; for his pictures, the *abandon* of which would have shocked

Mr. Spence more than ever, became instantly the vogue, and brought him speedy fame and fortune. For both of these he persisted in considering himself indebted to me. I never ventured to run the risk of wounding his sensibilities by offering him anything for the portrait, although in a merchantable sense its value was excessive.

I have not spoken of my Aunt Agnes; but up to this time there was little to be said of her. She kept up the even tenor of her ways, which included a repellent air toward me for long after my father's death. She might have forgotten and forgiven the past, but in my choice of Aunt Helen as a companion I had added insult to injury. There was no open breach of course, but our relations were not cordial. I tried at times to ameliorate the situation by sending her presents, and trying to let her see when we met that I was still studious and anxious to lead a sober life. But all in vain. She was resolute in the belief that to have refused an offer of marriage from such a man as Mr. Spence was inconsistent with a serious desire for self-improvement. She doubtless was abetted in this view by Miss Kingsley, who continued to be intimate at her house despite her increasing appropriation of

Mr. Spence. The philosopher was said to be more and more under her thrall every day, as I was informed by Mr. Fleisch whom I invited to several of my receptions. He told me he was himself no longer in harmony with Mr. Spence, or rather that the master could not afford to pay him a sufficient salary to warrant him in devoting his entire time to the doctrine of Moderation. His condensed music had not sold, and he had been forced, in order to support his wife and child (for he was married now), to adopt the old system of composition, and to give music lessons. This had caused a coolness on the part of Mr. Spence, who, as Mr. Fleisch expressed it, wished to have all or none. But though he was no longer the chief disciple, he held the master in the profoundest regard and affection. He assured me, with tears in his eyes, that nothing but the stress of absolute want could have induced him to sacrifice artistic truth to expediency, and that he stole hours from sleep that he might continue to carry on his investigations still. Here again I was able to be of some service, for I introduced Mr. Fleisch as a competent and conscientious musical instructor to a number of my friends, who seemed to find him all that I described. He played several of his pieces at my house with much *éclat*, even including one of those which illustrated Moderation. But I noticed as he became more popular and prosperous that he seemed content to adhere to the conventional methods, and to avoid allusion to his former hobbies.

Though I sent cordial invitations to Mr. Spence to lecture at my receptions, he invariably declined. I sometimes fancied that it might be because I did not extend them to Miss Kingsley also. I judged from what I saw in the newspapers, as well as from what Mr. Fleisch told me, that the number of his followers was diminishing in spite of his most earnest efforts, and that Miss Kingsley was now his only really devoted supporter. The knowledge of this counteracted my scruples against her so far that I sent an invitation to them both, with the assurance that Mr. Spence's lecture should be the feature of the occasion. They accepted, not altogether to my surprise, and I did my best to select an appreciative audience. Mr. Spence looked worn and dispirited I thought, but as he warmed to his theme the light in his eyes seemed as vivid as ever. The sweetness of his tones was however unfortunately impaired by a heavy cold, and though I, being familiar with the lecture, — "Tension and Torpor of the Nerves," — felt some of my old enthusiasm, it was soon evident to me that the majority of his listeners were bored. The appearance of Miss Kingsley likewise created an impression that reacted on the philosopher. She was very much overdressed, and made a marked effort to carry the assembly by storm. She played the double rôle of a would-be arch coquette and hero-worshipper, and while chanting the talent of the lecturer, omitted no effort to secure admiration on her own account. There are always a few men who are amused for the moment by this sort of thing, but I could see the eye-glasses of the censors raised wonderingly, and the turned shoulders grow colder, as the evening advanced. I was sorry for them both, even for her; and not many days after, I wrote Mr. Spence a long letter, in which I referred to the great influence in the way of discipline which I felt his instruction had had upon me, and inclosed a check for a considerable sum, which I asked him to accept as a contribution towards endowing a school where lectures should be delivered on the leading features of Moderation. I cannot say that I did this without some scruples, on the score that I no longer had much faith in the soundness of any of his ideas, but I condoned the weakness with my conscience by debiting the amount to charity. After all, he could not do much harm by his teachings, and I hated to think that a man so earnest as he should know the bitterness of total failure.

But my kind intentions met a cruel rebuff. On the following morning I received a formal note in Miss Kingsley's handwriting, which stated that Mr. Spence had desired her to say that it was impossible for him to accept the money, and that she was my " obedient servant, Lucretia Kingsley." My attention was called by a friend the same day to a long item in the " Sunday Mercury," which while extolling the lecture of Mr. Spence at my house, and announcing that among the guests was the "authoress Miss Kingsley, who wore, etc." contained a disagreeable comment on what was called "the lavish luxury and lack of discriminating reverence for the best sentiments of the day, which characterized the principal parlors."

The next time I went to see Aunt Agnes I received an explanation of this conduct, though my name had appeared once or twice before during the past few years in uncomplimentary paragraphs. She upbraided me at once with a renewed attempt to divert the attention of Mr. Spence from his labors to myself. Miss Kingsley had come to her with tears in her eyes, and described the Babylonian influences by which I had sought to seduce him. He had gone, she said, at the call of duty to accomplish what good he might, but never in the whole course of his professional experience had his words fallen on a more flinty and barren soil. And then, as if it were not enough to flaunt in the face of my old master the extravagances most hostile to the theories of which he was the advocate, I had sought to tempt him with money to become a perpetual presence at my immoderate receptions.

"Bah!" exclaimed Aunt Agnes in the ardor of her indignation, as she finished the account of Miss Kingsley's narrative,—"bah! Trying to lead a sober life! Tell *me!* I hear on all sides that your house has become a hot-bed of all that is worldly and luxurious in the city. And not content with that, you are scheming to corrupt the one who in this money-worshipping age is faithful to principle. I am almost disposed to say for the last time, 'Go your own ways, and never come near me again.'"

"Do not say that yet, Aunt Agnes. Wait a

little," I answered, genuinely moved by the distress of the old lady.

"If I were to wait until doomsday it would be still the same. You are no longer a child; and though you have Harlan blood in your veins, I am beginning to feel that I have wasted my best affections on a worthless subject. If you were my own daughter, I could not have been more unhappy on your account. Thank Heaven! I shall soon be in my grave."

I left the house feeling very much like crying, for the mood of Aunt Agnes was less defiant and more pitiful than usual. It seemed as though her iron spirit had yielded at last to the repeated opposition of an unkind world. And of those who had resisted her wishes and commands I was certainly among the chief. I had tried, was trying now, to live what she liked to call a sober life,—but all in vain, so far as winning her approval. Was there no way in which I could make her happy, and smooth the stern frown from her features before she died? I would certainly make the endeavor; and under the influence of this determination I revolved with a freshened interest as I went along the street the circumstances of a curious incident that had befallen me a week ago at Mr. Chelm's office. So absorbed was I that I did not notice the approach of Mr. Spence and Miss Kingsley until they were close upon me. I bowed with politeness; but though the philosopher hesitated, he turned his pale face away and looked in another direction. As for Miss Kingsley, she regarded me with a cold and haughty stare, as though we had never met.

II.

THE incident to which I have vaguely alluded was the result of an arrangement between Mr. Chelm and myself, that the door connecting our offices should be left ajar during the visits of his clients, except where privacy was important. In the latter case he was very careful, of course, to close it; but unless he did so I had his permission to listen to what was said. This soon became my favorite diversion, and I even came to the office for the purpose on other days than my usual one. A great many strange people came to consult Mr. Chelm, and I thus picked up a stock of miscellaneous information about business matters as well as some new ideas regarding human nature. Sometimes when the visitors seemed particularly interesting I would venture to peep round the corner or through the crack of the door, so as to catch a glimpse of them. Afterward Mr. Chelm often told me more about them, and in instances where pecuniary aid could be of service allowed me to come to the rescue; for there were numerous persons who resorted to him for relief, knowing that he was a charitable man who had helped others. If he had the leisure, he always lent a sympathetic ear to their stories, and if he could not aid them was uniformly kind and considerate.

I was struck by the number of applicants for employment. "Give us something to do, and we can get along. We want work, not money," was the too frequent petition, for it was just this class of persons whom Mr. Chelm found it most difficult to assist. So many of them too were educated and intelligent young men and women, unaccustomed to hardships and to shift for themselves, driven out of work by the continued hardness of the times. For nearly five years business had been at a stand-still, Mr. Chelm told me, and as a consequence property had depreciated sadly in value, and an immense amount of distress been caused among people of moderate means. To many a tale of destitution I thus listened with tears in my eyes, and on more than one occasion was able to procure at least temporary occupation for the sufferers.

One morning as I was thus sitting hoping for some client to arrive, I saw through the half open door a young man dressed in the height of fashion, *bien ganté, bien chaussé*, and attended by the very ugliest bull-terrier it had ever been my lot to gaze on, enter Mr. Chelm's office. I had by this time learned to divine usually the errands of clients before they began to speak, and I made up my mind that this handsome young dandy — for he was extremely good-looking to boot — must be the heir to some large estate which he wished to intrust to the care of Mr. Chelm, or that he had got entangled with an actress, and was in search of legal aid to release him from the meshes of the net. In either event I expected to have the door closed in my face, and the stranger's secret to remain sealed from me forever. I placed my chair however so that I should be screened from observation and yet within ear-shot, prepared to see and listen as long as should be possible.

The visitor drew a card from a very dainty case and laid it on Mr. Chelm's desk.

"My name is Prime, sir, — Francis Prime. I have come to consult you on a business matter."

"Pray sit down, Mr. Prime. What is it I can do for you?"

"You knew my father, I think?"

"Ralph Prime, of New York? Most assuredly. I had a high regard for him."

"I am his only son. He died, as you may be aware, five years ago in reduced circumstances, because he preferred to remain honest. An odd erratic choice, was it not?"

"I was sorry to hear he had been unfortunate," answered Mr. Chelm quietly.

"Yes, sir, paradoxical as it may seem, my father was an honest man. One might have supposed his only son would inherit that trait, if nothing else. But it must have skipped a generation. I am not what I seem. I am a sham." He sat in silence for some minutes stroking his mustache.

"I judge that you have got into some difficulty, Mr. Prime. If so, I am very sorry to hear it. Be frank with me, and as your father's friend I will do what I can for you. But as a lawyer I must ask you to conceal nothing." So saying Mr. Chelm made a move as if to close the door.

"Pray, do not trouble yourself, sir. My story is already known to so many people that privacy is immaterial. Let me, instead, ask permission to light a cigarette, — that is, if you do not object to smoking and are sufficiently at leisure to hear me to the end."

"Certainly. Make it a cigar and I will join you; and pray try one of these if you will, for my time is quite at your disposal," answered Mr. Chelm, who it was evident to me was amused and puzzled by his visitor.

"Thank you." He settled himself comfortably in his chair, and after a preliminary puff, said: "I am no ordinary felon. I am even not, strictly speaking, amenable to the laws. I am however, as I have told you already, a sham. The world believes me to be a young fellow of fortune, whose only concern is with the cut of his coat and the smile of his mistress. The world for once is in error. I am nothing of the sort. Appearances are against me, I admit. Even you I fancy were deceived. No, my dear sir, while every one judges me to be a mere butterfly of fashion, I am an idealist at heart. And the worst of it is that no one will believe me. All that I want is a chance, an opportunity to prove I am that which I claim; but nobody will give it to me. If I venture to suggest that I am in earnest, the statement excites sneers or ridicule. For nearly two years I have been trying to find something to do, and without success. I have exhausted my own city, and have now come to yours. Your name was familiar to me as one which my father respected, and it occurred to me to tell you my story. I am quite prepared to be informed that there are a thousand applicants for every vacancy, and that such a case as mine is not especially deserving. In one sense of the word you would be right; there are others who suffer more acutely than I, but few who suffer more unjustly. And the whole cause is to be found in a single phrase, — I am a gentleman."

"You are indeed to be pitied," said Mr. Chelm, with an amused laugh.

"And what is more, it is not my fault. I am not responsible for it; I was born so. My case is precisely opposite to that of most of my contemporaries. They find it easy enough to get occupation, but very difficult to be gentlemen; I know how to behave like a gentleman, but can find nothing to do. Gentlemen are evolved, not made. Would to Heaven I had been consulted on the subject! But I awoke one day and found myself what I am. Let me rehearse to you briefly my qualifications. I was sent to school abroad, and was graduated from college at home. I speak fluently three modern languages besides my own, and have a bowing acquaintance with two dead ones. I have read widely enough in history, political economy, literature, science, and music to be superficial. I can write verses, play on the piano and flute, fence, flirt, and lead the cotillon. All this the public seem to recognize and give me credit for; but when I ask them to take me seriously, as they would the veriest beggar in the street, the frivolous look incredulous and giggle, and the practical frown and point me to the door. And why? Simply,—and this will, it may be, anticipate your criticism,—simply because I wear well-fitting clothes, address a lady with gallantry, and change my coat for dinner. Let me add at once, if you have no assistance to offer as to how I shall find employment except to go from office to office with a long face and baggy trousers, I must respectfully decline to take the step. It has become a matter of pride with me: I draw the line there. Call it volatile, foolish, obstinate, what you will,—I propose to be a gentleman to the last. I will starve with a smile on my face and a flawless coat on my back, though it be my only one. As I have said, gentlemen are evolved, not made; and we owe it to our sons to keep up the standard of the race. They will not even allow, sir, that I am an American. I am received with scorn, and denied my birthright, not only by those to whom I apply for work, but by the Arabs of the street and the public press. I am not complaining; I am merely stating the facts of the case. They even cast Ike in my teeth, — Ike the imperious, beautifully ugly Ike," he added, stooping down to pat the bull-terrier, who showed his teeth and growled affectionately. "Now, Mr. Chelm, you have my story. I am in earnest. Will you help me?"

"I can understand your difficulties to some extent, Mr. Prime, and am not altogether without sympathy for you," began the lawyer gravely, after a short reflection. "The times are hard for everybody undeniably, and especially for young men in your position. It is a comparatively easy matter to draw a cheque to alleviate distress, but finding work for anybody to-day is next to impossible. However, as one can never tell what may turn up, let me ask you a blunt question. What are you fit for? What can you do?"

"Here again, sir, the world would tell you that I was fit for nothing except to play the lute beneath a lady's window. But if you will believe me, I am not without business knowledge. Gentleman as I am, I have long cherished an ambition to become a merchant prince (it is well to aspire high), — a genuine merchant-prince, however, and not the counterfeit article who accumulates millions for his children to squander. I have views upon the subject. I am an idealist, as I have told you, and there was a time when I thought my father very rich, and that I should be able to carry out my theories. Since then I have resolved to win back before I die the fortune he lost; and with a view to that I devote several hours in each day (if this should be breathed abroad, my reputation for consummate emptiness might suffer) to the study of exports and imports, markets and exchanges, and all that relates to commercial affairs. You asked me what I am fit for, Mr. Chelm. My father was a banker. I should like to follow in his footsteps. But supplicants cannot be choosers. Procure me a clerkship in any line of business, and I shall try to prove myself worthy of your patronage."

"Humph! I wish I could help you, with all my heart. But, frankly, I know of nothing at the moment. Bankers are discharging their clerks, not engaging new ones. I will make inquiries however, and see if it is possible to do anything for you. You have applied to all your friends in New York, you say, without avail?"

"Entirely. The few who have any faith in my professions are powerless to give me employment."

"Let me see: to-day is Wednesday. Can you call again on Saturday, Mr. Prime? Mind, I promise nothing. In fact, I have every reason to believe that I shall be unsuccessful."

The appointment thus made was due to my touching the electric bell in my office, — a signal agreed upon as an indication of my desire to assist any applicant for aid. Accordingly, when I entered Mr. Chelm's room after his visitor was gone, I was greeted with a bantering smile.

"How now, my fair philanthropist! What scheme have you to relieve the plight of this knight-errant?"

"In the first place," I said, "who is he? Do you believe his story? What sort of a person was his father?"

"Three questions in one breath! The last is the easiest to answer. This young man's father was one of the wealthiest bankers in New York fifteen years ago. I knew him well: a man who was the very soul of honor, shrewd and liberal in his business notions, and in his bearing the pattern of a finished gentleman, — one of your genuine aristocrats; and, like his son, a bit of a dandy. He came to grief, as so many of us do, through misplaced confidence. Certain parties whom he trusted implicitly made a wreck of his entire fortune. It was said at the time that he might have saved a large portion of it, had he been willing to take advantage of a legal technicality as against his creditors. But, as his son said, he preferred to remain honest. He died not many years ago, and left this boy very little, I fancy, but an untarnished name. Of the son I know really nothing. I have never seen him before. He is not unlike his father in appearance, and is even more fastidious in his dress. That may be from bravado, of course. What he says about gentlemen not having a fair chance in this country has a certain amount of truth in it."

"A great deal of truth, it seems to me," I answered.

"Very likely. But it is to be borne in mind that the so-called gentlemen have a heavy score against them in the past. They have had their innings; and now that they are out, democracy is not disposed to let them off too easily. The sins of the forefathers being visited on the children is a proverb as stable as the hills in its logical results."

"Yes. But do you not think it is cruel to turn the cold shoulder on a man merely because he dresses well?"

"Undoubtedly. But they have themselves to blame for it. The world has not yet got accustomed to the idea that a man with a flawless coat on his back means to do anything. Not so very long ago such a thing was unknown. I am willing to admit that when the gentlemen consent to work, they make the best workers; but the burden of evidence, as we lawyers say, is on them."

"The world refuses to believe because it is envious. There is n't one of the business men who decline to give Mr. Prime a chance who would n't give half his fortune to be like him if he could."

"You are a philosopher as well as a philanthropist, young lady, I see. You may not be far wrong. But if Mr. Prime knew what a champion he has, he would cease to despair. You asked, I think, if I believed his story. It is quite evident what your opinion is," said Mr. Chelm, with a laugh.

"Very well then, I do believe it; and I want to help him."

"Romance against the lawyers, ha! ha!"

"I am a very determined young person when I make up my mind. You cannot laugh me out of it, Mr. Chelm."

"Heaven forbid! But what do you propose to do?"

"Give him a chance."

The lawyer rubbed his chin reflectively. "I am perfectly willing to resign in his favor, but otherwise I know of no vacancy either in your or my gift to fill," he said with a smile.

"I cannot spare you yet. I have another plan."

"And that?"

"A very romantic one, as you have predicted. I propose to set him up in business."

"As a gentleman?"

"He is that already. No, as a banker."

"Indeed!"

"What do you think of my idea?"

"I have heard only the beginning of it. It is natural enough to feel the inclination to set a handsome young man up as a banker; but I fail to comprehend yet the details of the scheme."

"I shall leave them to you."

"To me? But I regret to say, Miss Harlan, that I know of no banking-house at present that would employ the services of this embryo merchant-prince."

"Oh, but you don't or you won't understand

me. What I propose is to found a banking-house, and furnish the capital myself."

"What!" Mr. Chelm leaned back in his chair and laughed heartily. "This is romance with a vengeance. Would I were twenty-five, and in search of occupation! And what, pray, is to be the name of the new concern?— Harlan and Prime; or Virginia Harlan and Company? I am confident it will be a partnership for life."

"Francis Prime and Company, of course. I will not submit to be laughed at, Mr. Chelm. This is a serious business matter."

"Oh, most certainly! Thoroughly business-like in every sense! My dear young lady, if you expect me to preserve my legal gravity you must not be so humorous; it is beyond the self-control of even a fusty conveyancer. And what part in this financial idyl am I expected to play!"

"You are to arrange it all. I am to furnish the money, and remain strictly incognito. That is the first and essential condition I impose."

"What! Mr. Prime is not to know the name of his benefactress?"

"On no account whatever!"

"He will be sure to search the earth until he finds her."

"Not if he be made to believe she is ancient and homely. Besides, how is he to know it is a woman?"

"Forgive me, Miss Harlan, but no one except a woman could invent such a project. It fairly takes my breath away. How much of your capital do you propose to embark in the enterprise,—the whole four millions?"

"No, Mr. Chelm, I am not utterly irrational yet. That is one of the points I mean to leave to your discretion. I merely insist that he shall not be scrimped. I do not think, however, that I care to advance over two hundred and fifty thousand dollars."

"Two hundred and fifty thousand dollars? And still you talk of discretion!"

"Is not that enough?"

"Enough! Why, certainly not. If you are bent upon the plan, at least put it through handsomely, Miss Harlan. Let him have a cool million at once, and be done with it."

"I know, of course, that this must seem very quixotic to you as a business man, Mr. Chelm," I continued after a moment's reflection. "Very likely you think I am merely jesting. But I am not. I am perfectly serious. I want to help Mr. Prime. I was very much interested by what he said, and I believe he is in earnest. The plan that I have just suggested seems to me entirely feasible. Even supposing that I lose a couple of hundred thousand dollars, what then? It is a year's income at the worst; whereas, on the other hand, if the scheme prospers, and he turns out to be "—

"A merchant prince," interrupted Mr. Chelm.

"Yes, a merchant prince, as I believe he will," —

"You will be married, and be happy ever after, as in other fairy stories."

"Nothing of the sort, Mr. Chelm. My conclusion of the affair is much less sentimental. In case events result as I hope and predict, I shall be thankful that I have given him a chance to put his theories into practice. You may remember that he said he had theories regarding the use a rich man should make of his money."

"It strikes me you are willing to pay pretty dear for the probable value of the information, even if matters turn out as you expect. But the money is yours, Miss Harlan, not mine; and if you are resolved upon being generous in this wholesale way, it is not for me to complain. We lawyers get conservative as we grow older, and any romance that may have been in us dries up, like the sap in trees that have begun to outlast their usefulness. We know how hard it is to earn an honest living; and when we see any one in whom we have an interest developing a taste for imprudent speculations, we instinctively utter a protest. Still, as you say, it is but a year's income; and maybe the cheapest way in the end to teach you reason is to humor this expensive fancy. If the money is lost, you will never miss it; while, assuming that this young man is all your imagination paints him, I know of nothing that would give me greater pleasure than to see you happily married. That is a romance to which I would say 'Amen' with all my heart."

"Thank you very much, Mr. Chelm. But I will not obtain your connivance on any such terms. If you regard this as other than a purely business enterprise, I warn you that you will be wofully disappointed."

"I shall have to take my chance of being right, just as you are going to take yours. But come now, since you insist upon my treating this matter seriously, what is it that you wish me to do?"

"Everything, Mr. Chelm."

"Even to giving away the bride? You must promise me that, eh! Miss Harlan?"

"With pleasure."

"It is a bargain then. Command my services as you will, — I wish I could say my capital also. But unfortunately I cannot afford to toss away my hundreds of thousands like some people. But that is an aside. Tell me what you wish me to do. I am all ears."

"To begin with, when Mr. Prime returns on Saturday, I should like you to inform him that you happened by chance to mention his predicament to a friend of yours."

"Of which sex?"

"That is entirely immaterial. But if he should happen to inquire, I shall depend on you to preserve my incognito. You must even fib a little, if it is necessary."

"Mercy on us! This romantic young philanthropist talks of fibbing, as if it were the most simple thing in life. No, Mademoiselle, we lawyers never fib. If we are ever obliged to forsake the narrow pathway of truth, we tell a square, honest lie. But this is positively my last interruption."

"You are to tell him that this friend of yours was very much interested in his endeavors to find something to do, and sympathized with his determination to wear a smile on his face and avoid baggy trousers to the last. That I — I mean of course the friend — am willing to give him the chance for which he asks to prove himself a man, by placing in your hands a sufficient sum to found a banking-house of undoubted solvency. He is to have complete control of this money, on which he may pay interest if he chooses, in order to satisfy your business scruples, Mr. Chelm; but he need never pay it back unless he wishes to do so, — the particulars of all which you will understand how to arrange better than I can tell you. Some day in the dim future, when he has realized his ambition, — for don't imagine for an instant, Mr. Chelm, that I expect him to make a fortune all at once, — he may return the original loan if he sees fit. I shall be an old woman then, and should, it may be, have less objection to being known as his benefactress than at present. Let me see: is there anything else to say? As to the name of the firm, it ought to be Francis Prime and Company, I presume; but the 'company' must be a man of straw. He is to receive no outside help, not even from you. There, I think I have made my wishes sufficiently plain."

"You do not desire him to give security for whatever you may advance? Not a very business-like arrangement. But as for that, the whole scheme is the most Utopian I ever heard of. These women, these women! It makes a prudent man tremble to think what would become of the universe if they had full sway! But I must submit, I suppose. I have given my word."

"I fear he has no security to offer unless it be Ike, the beautifully ugly Ike; Ike the imperious! Do you suppose he would part with the animal? I took rather a fancy to him, did n't you Mr. Chelm?"

"Nay, there I shall put down my foot. I will have no dogs in this office. 'Love me, love my dog' is a maxim to which I could not subscribe even in your case. No, unbusiness-like as it is, I prefer to make the loan without security."

It may be easily imagined that during the next few days I was on tiptoe with expectation. Let it be said at once, that I was quite aware that I was about to commit what might fairly be considered a folly by prudent-minded people. The chances of my goose proving a swan were altogether too slight to justify the extravagance I proposed. But despite this I never once wavered in my resolution, nor suffered doubt to mar the mirror of fancy in which I chose to behold my protégé fulfilling the ample measure of his ambition in the years to come. What an absorbing interest it would be to me to watch from behind my mask the progress he made! If he proved successful, I could feel that part of the creating power was mine; for had I not trusted him? Let a man realize that there is some one who has faith in him, and the battle is half won. Even suppose he were to prove the recreant and the impostor predicted, the world would not be able to jeer at me; I could hug my wretched secret, and none would be the wiser. Decidedly, I was to be envied in the acquisition of this new interest. It would be almost like having a double self, for was not my hero pondering over the same questions that were constantly in my thoughts, — how a rich man was to spend his money? With this difference, however: his ideas were already settled, whereas mine were in process of formation. I was to share with him my fortune, and he would enlighten me in turn. Perhaps also there was a shade of irony in my reflections, and I was eager to see if he would find the rôle of a merchant-prince so easy to play as he seemed to fancy. Then, too, there was a delightful element of uncertainty and mystery about it all. I was original; I was not copying every one else. Although of Mr. Prime in a personal sense I scarcely thought at all, there was a romantic flavor to the episode that stirred my imagination.

So gay and light-hearted did I feel that Aunt Helen noted it, and alluded to the fact with pleasure as we sat together on the Friday evening previous to Mr. Prime's return.

"I have good reason to be. I feel very happy to-night. I could dance until morning, or do anything equally frivolous and erratic," I answered mysteriously. She looked up with an anxious expression. "No, Aunt Helen dear, I am not engaged. It is nothing so dreadful as that. It is merely that I think I may have found my mission at last."

"Mission! What does the child mean? Don't tell me," she cried with a sudden access of horror, "that you are going out to convert the Indians, or to do any peculiar thing like that. That would be the last straw!"

"Try again," I said laughing.

"You gave me a scare, Virginia! You are such a strange girl, that, though you are more like other people than you used to be, I can never feel quite sure of you. If it isn't that you are engaged, or going to do something odd, what is it, dear?"

"Nothing, Aunt Helen. I was merely romancing a little, that's all. As you say, I am a strange girl, and very likely what I am thinking about is all a delusion, and may never come to anything. I may wake up any morning and find it is a dream. But let your mind rest easy; I am not contemplating anything that will isolate me from society."

"I should hope not, I am sure, after your last experience;" and I heard her mutter to herself as I went out of the room, — "Mission? Why does she want to bother her head about a mission? I shall never feel perfectly safe until I see her well married."

III.

I HAD decided to be present at the second interview between Mr. Chelm and Mr. Prime, for several reasons. I was curious to have another look at my beneficiary, and I had an impression that Mr. Chelm might feel his legal conscience prick him, and so spoil the plot, if I were not within earshot. When the interview took place, however, the lawyer took a mild revenge by toying with his visitor a little at first, as though about to give an unfavorable answer; and I shall never forget Mr. Prime's expression when the true state of the case was made known to him. After sitting in silence for a moment as though endeavoring to grasp the facts, he gave a short incredulous laugh, and stooping down to pat Ike, said nervously, —

"Is this a joke? A ghastly practical joke?"

"It sounds like one, doesn't it?" said Mr. Chelm; and he grinned from ear to ear. "I fancy, though, that you are not in a mood to be trifled with. No, you have fallen on your feet this time, young man. What I have told you is all true."

"Do you mean to say that your friend wishes to advance me two hundred and fifty thousand dollars to found a banking-house?"

"Precisely."

"But I have no security to offer."

"I have already told you that no security will be required."

"Excuse me — eh — but is your friend of sound mind?"

"I don't wonder you ask, ha! ha! But I am compelled to answer yes. My friend is a philanthropist. That may make matters clearer."

"It is like a fairy story, isn't it Ike? Let me rehearse the conditions again, so as to be sure I am not dreaming. With this loan, which I shall never be called on to pay back unless I choose, I am to establish in New York the house of Francis Prime and Company. I am to devote my energies, first, to becoming abnormally rich; and after that simple result is accomplished, to carry out the theories I have as to how one in that position should live. Meanwhile, I am to pledge my word never to divulge the circumstances of this interview, and on no pretence whatever to seek to discover the name of the person to whom I owe my good fortune. Have I omitted anything?"

"You have stated the case exactly."

"Humph! I should like to ask a single question. Is my benefactor a man or a woman?"

"Another question like that would justify me in withdrawing the offer," answered Mr. Chelm with gravity. "My client wishes to have no identity whatever. Come, sir, my time is precious. I await your decision."

"The proposal is so sudden and unexpected. To ascend in a twinkling from the depths of despair to the summit of hope, leaves one a trifle bewildered. But you are right. I have no claim on your time. You want an answer."

He laughed again in a nervous manner, and stroked Ike.

"I do not wish to hurry you unduly. I have a letter to write, which will take me a few minutes. Think the matter over until I have finished."

"Thank you. I will. But since, I have imposed upon your good nature so far, do me one more kindness, Mr. Chelm. What is your own opinion in this matter? Do you advise me to accept?"

I listened eagerly for his reply. It was in his power to spoil all.

"Really, I feel embarrassed how to answer.

As I have already implied to you, the proposition strikes me, as a lawyer, as being the most preposterous piece of extravagance I ever heard suggested. I will tell you frankly that I tried my utmost to dissuade my client from making it. It is thoroughly unbusiness-like and absurd. That is my view of the matter from a professional standpoint."

"I see," said Mr. Prime.

"But," continued Mr. Chelm, — and here he stopped and gave an amused chuckle, — "it is a rare chance for a young man, a rare chance. My client will never mind the loss of the money, and would feel genuine disappointment, I know, if you were to decline. This being the case, and feeling as I do that you are in earnest in your desire to succeed despite your aristocratic tendencies, I am tempted on the whole to urge you to accept the good fortune which is thrust upon you. It is for my client's sake as much as for your own that I advise this, for I can see that she has set her heart—"

He stopped short. There was a dead pause, and I felt the blood rush to my cheeks.

"Well!" he exclaimed, "I have let the cat out of the bag with a vengeance this time. A lawyer, too. Pshaw! It is too bad!"

"That settles it," said Mr. Prime, quietly; "I cannot accept now at any rate. It would not be fair to your client."

"Not accept? Of course you will accept. Nonsense, nonsense! It is all my fault, and you shall have the money now if I have to pay it out of my own pocket. Besides," said Mr. Chelm with voluble eagerness, "there is very little harm done after all; and to prevent misunderstanding, I may as well make a clean breast of it. My client is an eccentric maiden-lady of sixty-five, with a lot of distant relatives who bother her life out while waiting for her to die. I am her only intimate friend, but even I cannot prevent her from doing all sorts of queer things in her taste for sentimentality. You see, poor woman, when she was very young she had a lover of just about your age (she wears his portrait perpetually in a locket about her neck), who died. He was in business, and doing very well. Several times already, on this account, she has helped young men who were in straits; and when I told her your story, and what you were ambitious to do, she clapped her withered old hands together and said, 'I will give him a chance, Mr. Chelm, I will give him a chance! He reminds me of my Tom.' And that is how it came to pass. There is the long-and-short of the matter. Accept? To be sure you will accept. It is all my fault. I will make it right with her. It would break her heart if you did not. So, no more words about it. I have all the necessary papers ready."

Mr. Prime was patting Ike more abstractedly than ever. As for me, I sat aghast and overwhelmed. The next few seconds seemed an eternity.

"Well, young man?"

"Please to write your letter, Mr. Chelm, and give me time to think."

"Not a bit of it! The letter can wait. Say you accept, and be done with it!"

"Very well then, I accept. We are gentlemen of fortune, Ike, and you shall have a new silver collar to-morrow."

It is not necessary to describe the details of the interview further. An hour elapsed before the final arrangements were made and Mr. Prime left the office. He was to start in business as soon as possible, and make frequent reports of his progress to Mr. Chelm. Meanwhile I sat within hearing distance, and occasionally took a peep at them from my coign of vantage. I could perceive from Mr. Chelm's manner that he was pleased with the tone and alertness of the other in putting matters into shape. He had shown me beforehand certain letters which he had received in answer to inquiries made regarding Mr. Prime. In these he was spoken of as a young man of irreproachable character but strong social tastes, which, while consistent with his own statement of what the world thought of him, did not serve to re-assure Mr. Chelm as to the success of my experiment. So it was consoling to me to see his expression continue benignant as he listened to the young banker's notions.

When at last Mr. Prime was gone, I indulged my hilarity freely at my friend's expense. "A lawyer, too!" I cried, when I could speak. "Your reputation in my eyes is ruined forever."

"I have no excuse to offer. It was a dreadful slip, Miss Harlan."

"The slip was unpardonable of course; but it was an accident. No, what I refer to, Mr. Chelm, is the marvellous invention by which you sought to conceal it. I fully expected to see the floor open, and some demon carry you off amid smoke and sulphur."

"I never stick at a trifle like that," laughed he. "But did n't I do the thing well? He believed every word of it. And what is more, Miss Harlan," he added seriously, "it would have been a great pity to have let him decline. He is a likely young fellow. I smell weddingcake in the air already."

"You forget, Mr. Chelm," I answered, "that I am an eccentric maiden-lady of sixty-five. You have ruined any material there may have been out of which to manufacture a romance."

This turn of affairs took place a few days before the unpleasant scene with Aunt Agnes occurred, to which I have alluded, and I found that it absorbed my thoughts and tended to counteract the despondency produced by her displeasure and the injustice of her friends. All through the remainder of the season I awaited with eagerness the monthly reports sent by Mr. Prime. He was established, and cautiously feeling his way. But necessarily there was little to tell; a fortune cannot be made in a minute. However, I cherished every word of encouragement as so much vindication of my faith; and I came by degrees to feel as though Mr. Prime's new enterprise were my own business, and that my reputation for sagacity were dependent upon his success.

And yet, as I have already implied, Mr. Prime was nothing to me except so far as he represented an instrument of my will. It was not in him that I was interested half so much as in myself. In order to satisfy my curiosity, I even planned in the spring a trip to New York with Aunt Helen, and delighted my eyes with a glimpse of the sign-board over the spacious offices of Francis Prime and Company. But on that day it was veritably a glimpse that I got, for I was too timid to take a deliberate scrutiny of what I had come to see, owing to the fact that every one I met stared at me; and then too I was momentarily upset by perceiving over the way just opposite, in great gilt letters, the rival sign, as it seemed to me, of " Roger Dale, Banker and Broker." Mr. Dale I had not seen for several years, but I knew that he was living in New York, where he had not long before married an heiress of obscure antecedents, according to rumor. That it was he I had little doubt; and though the fact of his having an office in the same street could not of course affect, either for evil or otherwise, the interests of my protégé, I had an indefinable feeling of dread at perceiving they were so near to one another. It was therefore doubly necessary for me to be careful in my subsequent expeditions down-town, not only to dress in such a quiet unfashionable manner as not to attract the attention of passers, but so as to escape recognition from my former admirer.

After the first impression of unpleasantness I felt a little added zest on account of this element of risk, especially when on inquiry I learned that Roger Dale was rated as one of the most successful and enterprising of the younger banking firms in the city. I saw his advertisements in the newspapers, and gathered from current talk that he was doing a large and lucrative business. I was glad to know that he was happy and prosperous at last, for he had failed once before leaving home, though I never heard of it until a long while after; and under the influence of this mood any vestige of ill-will that may have been lurking in my mind died away, and I came to regard the rival sign with perfect equanimity from behind the thick veil by which I concealed my features. Instigated by a spirit of caution to make my disguise as complete as possible, I purchased at a cheap clothing-store some garments that did much towards rendering my personal appearance the very opposite of stylish. I even tried to give them a soiled and worn aspect, by means of experiments at home, so that I might pass for a female clerk or needy bushel-woman, and be free to pursue my investigations unobserved. In this guise I spent a number of days in wandering about the business streets of the city, attentive not only to what went on in the offices of Francis Prime and Company and Roger Dale, but to the countless sights and sounds of bustling trade, which I experienced now for the first time. At first I did not dare to appear too frequently in the street which was the centre of my interest, but a dangerous fascination led me to become bolder and more adventurous as I became familiar with the surroundings. From under the obscurity of arches and from behind pillars I noted daily who entered the doors of the new firm, and endeavored to get an idea of the amount of business that it transacted. In this respect I was somewhat disappointed, for although customers were by no means lacking, there was a dearth of patronage as compared with that enjoyed by the banking-house across the street. During the morning hours there was an incessant stream of people coming and going up and down the marble steps of the great building on the first floor of which were the offices of Roger Dale; and by far the larger proportion of this number went no farther, for I could see them through the broad plate-glass windows, chatting and grouped about a coil of tape that ran out with a snake-like movement into a basket on the floor. There were ladies too who drove up to the door in their carriages and were shown into the back office, and who when they came out again were attended by Mr. Dale himself, bowing obsequiously. He was stouter than when I saw him last, and quite bald; and he had a different suit of a prominent check-pattern for every day in the week. He seemed immensely popular with his customers, and was slapped by them on the back incessantly, and most of them he slapped back in return. But toward certain individuals he adopted a quite different style of behavior; for he listened to what they said with deference, gave them the most comfortable seat in the office, and opened the door for them when they went away. These I judged to be capitalists and men of influence, whose business he wished to secure. Some of them never came again, but others would return in the afternoon and be closeted with him for hours.

To all this I could not help giving attention, for it was forced on me, as I have indicated, by way of contrast to the style of business that was done by the firm to which my faith was pinned.

Indeed I felt badly sometimes, and wondered if it could be that my hero were lacking in enterprise and what the world calls "push." But as I observed more closely, I dismissed this suspicion as unjust; for I began to note that one or two of the grave, important-looking men whom Roger Dale treated with so much suavity, were much more frequent visitors over the way. Besides, the plate-glass windows were very small, and it was next to impossible to see what went on inside. Mr. Prime always stayed at his office until nearly six o'clock, and once or twice he was still at work at his desk when the darkness drove me home. In these afternoon hours the street was nearly deserted, and sometimes I ventured close up to the window and peered through. I could see him in a little inner office, writing and poring over papers and accounts. Once while I was thus occupied, a policeman greatly alarmed me by tapping me on the shoulder and observing roughly, "Now then, young woman, move on."

After this I felt the necessity of using more discretion; and lest this narration may prejudice the judicious too strongly against me, let it be said that I passed in all only some eight or ten days in this manner during the six weeks Aunt

Helen and I were in New York together. Perhaps, however, this was due somewhat to the difficulty I found in evading her eagle eye, for owing to the necessary changes in my dress I had to invent some excuse commensurate with such a dilapidated appearance. As excursions among the poor twice a week could not seem improbable, I let them account for the plain stuff-gown and unfashionable hat that I wore on the occasion of my down-town visits, and limited myself accordingly. Aunt Helen really shed tears at first because I looked so like a guy; but when I represented to her that it would be cruel to flaunt silks and satins in the faces of those to whom such luxuries were forbidden, to say nothing of the risk one ran of being insulted if gaudily attired, she withdrew her objections. "But only think," said she, "if any of your acquaintances should see you rigged out like that! It could not fail to strike the Honorable Ernest Ferroll as exceedingly peculiar at the best."

IV.

ALTHOUGH I had striven to keep our visit to New York a secret, it was hardly to be expected, in view of my quasi celebrity at home as a society character, coupled with my Aunt's eagerness for amusement, that our presence would long escape detection. As a fact, before the end of the first week we were inundated with invitations, many of which it was impossible to decline; and I finally gave up the struggle, and suffered myself to become a facile tool in the hands of my friends after night-fall, reserving merely the day-time for my financial investigations. I was the more willing to submit to this social demand, because I had a hope that I might meet with Mr. Prime at some of the houses to which we were asked. But though I constantly recognized, with a sense of danger that was yet delicious, faces that I had become familiar with down-town, his was never among them. I made no inquiries, but the mystery of his absence was finally explained.

"Miss Harlan," said my hostess to me at a brilliant dinner-party, "I had hoped to be able to present to you this evening my friend Mr. Francis Prime, who is altogether charming; but he writes me that he is not going anywhere this winter: he has in fact given himself up for the time being to business, and cannot break his rule even for me. Everybody is laughing over the idea of his doing anything except make himself agreeable. As he is n't here, let me tell you he is the worst flirt in town; and we all rather hope he won't succeed, for he fills his niche to perfection, — which is paying him a high compliment, I think. But there are other attractive men in the world besides Mr. Prime, and I am going to ask you, by and by, to tell me your opinion of our new Englishman, who is to take you in to dinner. He is only the Honorable Ernest Ferroll at present, but when his uncle dies he will be Duke of Clyde, my dear, and *on dit* he is looking for a wife."

I found the Honorable Ernest decidedly agreeable. He had a fine figure, was six feet high, with blue eyes and a luxuriant chestnut beard. In his thirty years he had lived and travelled everywhere, reserving the States, as he called them, for a final jaunt preparatory to settling down. He was making merely a flying trip through the sea-board cities after a preliminary canter at Newport, previous to doing California and some big hunting in the "Rockies;" but later he intended to return and spend a season in New York and Boston society. His name was, for the moment, on every one's lips, and there was much quiet maternal inquiry as to how long the old peer was likely to last; for the Honorable Ernest was said to be rather short of money.

"He has a fine forehead, and if one likes beards, his is certainly a handsome specimen," said Aunt Helen ruminantly, as we were driving home. "I have no fancy for them myself, but it is always possible to shave them off; that's one comfort."

I divined of whom she was speaking, but made no response.

"How did you like him, Virginia?"

"Mr. Ferroll? I found him very entertaining," I replied.

"I thought he seemed decidedly impressed by you. He scarcely kept his eyes off you all through dinner. I don't blame him, for you were looking your best. Duchess of Clyde! You might do worse, Virginia. They say he is anxious to marry."

"So Mrs. Tremaine informed me."

"Did she really? That was very amiable of her, especially as you are a stranger, and there must be plenty of girls in whom she is interested, who are setting their caps for him. I could not help thinking at dinner what a handsome pair you would make."

"One would suppose you were in earnest from your serious tone, Aunt Helen."

"And so I am, so I am, quite in earnest. Of course I should wish to know a little more definitely about him before anything final was arranged. But from what I hear, there can be no question in regard to his title. If there were the slightest suspicion of anything out of the way concerning it, he would never have been at Mrs. Tremaine's, who is a very particular woman, and knows what she knows. He seems, so far as I could judge, to be a manly, right-minded young man. He told me that he shot three tigers in India, and I observed that he took scarcely any wine at dinner. It won't do though, Virginia, to dilly-dally, for I am given to understand that he leaves in a fortnight for California, to explore the West. But he is coming back to spend several months next winter, and if you do not throw cold water on him now, he may feel disposed to run on to Boston, in spite of the efforts that will be made to keep him here."

"I feel very certain," said I, "that he will come to Boston for a few days, as he has letters to Aunt Agnes."

"To your Aunt Agnes? What do you mean, child?" In her astonishment I thought she was going to bounce out of the carriage.

"I don't wonder you are surprised. Yes, the first question he asked was if I were not the niece of Miss Agnes Harlan, of Boston. It seems that she and his father made an ocean passage together a great many years ago, when they were both young, and the acquaintance has been kept up by correspondence ever since."

"Mercy on us! Your Aunt Agnes has never said a word to me about it."

"The Honorable Ernest's father is quite literary, and has written one or two books on philosophy, his son says."

"That accounts for it, of course. Well, well! to think of your Aunt Agnes being intimate with one of the nobility, and having never mentioned the subject! I have always given her credit for being an agreeable woman at bottom, if one could only forget her eccentricities. But this is extremely fortunate for you, Virginia. To be sure, there is no knowing how your Aunt will receive him, she is so hostile to every one who is not as queer as herself. But she must see, if she is not a fool, what a very advantageous match this would be for you. It could do no harm just to drop Mr. Ferroll a hint to humor her a little, and seem fond of serious subjects at the start, for if she should happen to take it into her head to ask him to stay at her house it would be very convenient."

These sentiments were frequently reiterated by Aunt Helen during the remaining weeks of our visit, and it must be allowed that the attentions of the Honorable Ernest soon justified her urgency, seeing that she really believed it was a matter of vital importance for me to become the future Duchess of Clyde. Nor was I at all sure myself, that if nothing else turned up I might not be tempted by the brilliancy of such a position. Not that I thought about it quite so definitely; but I was conscious of the exceptional advantages incident to high rank in England, to the extent that I did not treat his gallantries with marked indifference. I let him reveal himself for what he was, which is not possible without a certain degree of intimacy. Beneath his conventional ways I discovered a great deal of energy and decision. He was well-read, and had his own opinions. On many of the days when I did not go down-town, I took strolls with him in the Park and elsewhere. We discussed all sorts and kinds of subjects. We did not often agree, but that rather added to the interest of our intercourse than otherwise. I was a curiosity to him, he said. He complained that I was too radical and visionary in my ideas, and that I was quite different from his conception of American girls. To be sure, he said, I was ready to do things, — that is, go to walk with him, and banish Aunt Helen when he called; but he had been told that American girls knew nothing about politics or any serious matters, and were principally interested in the study of their inner consciousness as affected by man; whereas I was perpetually taking issue with him on questions of government policy and pauperism, driving him into holes in regard to the value of an hereditary nobility and the dis-establishment of the English Church. Women at home were not like that, he said. The men told them what to believe, and they stuck to it through thick and thin; but voluntary feminine ratiocination was the rarest thing in the world among his countrywomen. As for himself, he was a conservative, — a conservative without money. Money was all he needed to build up the splendid estates of Clyde, which had been slowly decaying for this lack during two generations. His chief ambition was to retouch and refurbish the broad domain of his inheritance, so that its lordly manors, ivy-mantled abbeys, and green meadows might know again the peace, poetry, and prosperity of an ideal English home. There would then for the lord of Clyde be happiness and romance equalled by none on earth. For, eager to benefit his fellow-men, he would have within the radius of his own estate a hundred cabins to call in play his invention or humanity; and with one's conscience at rest, he said, could there be a purer joy than to wander with her of one's choice under the ancestral elms of old England, with the September moon o'erhead?

This was the Honorable Ernest's dream; but to realize it, he must make money. He had come to the States, so he told me when we grew more intimate, in order to seek it. There were great chances in the far West for a shrewd man with a little capital, and to find some investment that promised large returns was the real object of his journey thither. Already, even since his arrival in New York, he had done extremely well.

There was a smart (so he had heard him called) young fellow who had put him into several profitable speculations: very likely I might know him,— Roger Dale was his name; every one said he had made a lot of money, and was one of the coming men of Wall Street. I was kindly to consider this as a confidence, for he did not care to have it noised about that he was other than an idler here.

The Honorable Ernest Ferroll's attentions, as I have implied, grew apace from the evening of our introduction, and soon attracted remark. There was an instant recognition of the fitness of the match even from the most envious, and Aunt Helen was the recipient of numerous congratulatory innuendoes. The circumstance of his delaying the date of his journey a week confirmed the general impression of his serious views, and even I began to feel some pangs of conscience on the score of allowing him to fancy that if he did come to the point I should accept him eagerly. In contemplation of this emergency I felt that it was time for me to go home. We both would then have six months in which to think it over. When he should return from the West, it would be time enough for me to come to a decision as to whether I desired to re-gild the poetry of his English home. I was certain that if he insisted on an immediate answer my reply would be unfavorable. But I much preferred to defer any definite proposal; and accordingly, with all the tact at my command, I tried to avoid giving him an opportunity of being left alone with me for any length of time, without making it noticeable to him. Finally, as he seemed likely to become unmanageable despite my precautions, and as he put off again and again his day of departure, I resolved to take refuge in flight.

When I communicated this to Aunt Helen she said I was crazy. The idea of returning home just on the eve of realization seemed to her preposterous; she would not hear of it. But I was equally firm, and announced my intention of leaving on the morrow.

But before I went, I wished to have one more glimpse of the condition of the banking-house of Francis Prime and Company; and in order to make my scrutiny as thorough as possible I planned not to return until dark. I was curious to get a close look at my hero, and this seemed most feasible when he was leaving the office for the day. At that time there would be little likelihood of any one noticing me, if I stood by the door as he came out.

The afternoon passed without incident, save that I saw the Honorable Ernest Ferroll go into Mr. Dale's office, where he remained some time. He happened to meet me face to face on the street, but I justly had acquired by this time complete faith in my disguise. He betrayed no sign of recognition, and the flush that rose to my cheeks was a badge of quite unnecessary alarm. The hours slipped by, and the street grew still. The gas was lighted in the inner offices, and few but clerks, figuring up the profits or losses of the day, were left down-town. It was getting dark, and I was growing impatient. I sat down in the door-way of the building next adjoining, to rest. I had purposely made myself look as dilapidated as possible, and the natural presumption in the mind of any one would have been that I was friendless and needy, for I felt tired enough to make a weary air very natural at the moment.

As it chanced, my old enemy the policeman came sauntering by, and his cold eye fell on me with a chilling scrutiny. He stopped and said: —

"Did n't I tell you to move on, young woman? We don't want the likes of you loafing about here."

"I am tired and resting. I am waiting for some one," I answered, too much alarmed to take much account of my words.

"Yes, I dare say. He's forgotten to keep his engagement, and has gone home for the day. He asked me himself to tell you so. Come, move on, and don't let me see you hanging around any more, or I'll find an engagement for you that will last sixty days. Come, march!"

"Sir!" I exclaimed in a tone of indignation, having partially recovered my presence of mind, "what right have you to insult a lady? I tell you I have business here. If you don't instantly leave me, I will have you discharged to-morrow!"

"Do, my beauty! and lest you should over-sleep yourself in the morning, and not be on hand to keep your word, come with me now."

He reached out his hand to seize me by the arm, and all my fears returned. But at that instant I heard a voice, and to my mingled relief and consternation the face of Francis Prime appeared over my tormentor's shoulder.

"What is the matter, officer?"

"Nothing, your honor, except this here young woman. She's for reporting me, she is, and losing me my situation. But as I happen to have seen her congregating by herself mostly every day for the past fortnight around these offices, I thought I'd run her in as a disreputable lot, and we'd see who's who."

"Oh, sir! — Mr. Prime!" I cried, forgetting my discretion in the excitement of the moment, "don't let him take me off! What he says isn't true. I'm a lady — that is, a poor girl who's perfectly honest, and is trying to earn her living."

"A nice lady you are, trying to lose hard-working folks their situations!"

"You called me by name," said Mr. Prime. "Do you know me? Come here Ike!" The dog was sniffing around my feet.

"Yes, sir — no — that is, I have seen you come out of your office."

He looked at me searchingly, and turned to the policeman. "What was she doing when you arrested her?"

"Indeed, sir," I broke in, "I was merely sitting here resting myself, when this — this man spoke to me. I was doing nothing wrong."

"You hear what she says, officer. What is your charge against her?"

"Promiscuous and unlawful congregating by herself, your Honor. When a young woman as swears she's honest, goes peeking into other folks's windows after dark, I always has my suspicions, — as you would too, if you had been in the business as long as I have. It wa'n't more than a week ago that I caught her with her nose against that plate-glass window of yours, and I told her then to move on. But she did n't; and the next thing we shall be hearing some fine morning, that there's been breaking and entering done."

Frightened as I was, I could not help blushing.

"Why were you looking into my office?" said Mr. Prime. "It does n't seem a very serious offence," he added, turning to the officer.

"It ain't murder, and it ain't arson, that's flat," observed that functionary; "but we don't draw no such fine distinctions in our profession. If we did, the judges would have nothing to do."

The colloquy gave me time to think up an answer. I was in a tight place, and it would not do to mince matters. Mr. Prime turned back to me with an air of inquiry.

"I was wondering, sir, when I looked into your window, if there were any use in my applying for work."

"Are you in want?" he asked.

"I am trying to find a place. I am without

occupation at present. The times are so hard it is almost impossible for an honest girl to find anything to do. I only want a chance."

He looked at me with a closer interest. Of course my voice and my features, after the first impression produced by my needy dress, must have puzzled an observer so intelligent as Mr. Prime.

"I believe the girl's story," he said to the policeman. "I feel sure she is honest."

The man shrugged his shoulders. "A moment ago it was she was a lady, and waiting for somebody. But I ain't particular, if you are ready to go bail for the young woman. Of course I'm only doing my duty; and if you are satisfied, your Honor, don't blame me if you find your watch missing before you get home. I always keep a pair of twisters alongside of mine; and that's why I thought she might be safer with me than with you."

With this oracular utterance, the official turned on his heel and departed, to my intense relief. I was fairly overcome with dread and mortification, and my eyes fell under the interested look of my rescuer.

"You seem distressed and tired, poor girl. This street is no place for you at such an hour. You say you are in search of work?"

"Yes, sir," I answered faintly.

"Humph! Can you write?"

"Oh, yes, sir."

"Come to my office then, to-morrow morning, and I may be able to find something for you to do. And now go home as fast as you can. Stop, here is a trifle for your fare. Good-night."

He raised his hat in recognition of the grateful glance from my eyes. My cheeks had felt like live coals as I took the coin he held out to me. But I chose to continue the deception. It was harmless; and to disclose the fact that I was other than I seemed would only make matters worse. There was too, even while he was still present, an element of amusement to me in the whole affair, which when he was gone, and I knew that I was out of danger, speedily became predominant in my mind. Here was an opportunity sent by Providence to supervise my banking scheme without risk of discovery, if only I had the courage to take advantage of it. The idea pleased me the more I thought it over, for I had little doubt that Mr. Prime intended to find employment for me in his own office. I felt that it would amuse me immensely to become a female clerk for a few weeks and see the practical working of a business house, and above all others of this particular one. I felt sure that I could prove myself tolerably useful as well, thanks to my experience under Mr. Chelm; and there was no knowing what might come of it all if I should develop a taste for banking. The world's opinion to the contrary notwithstanding, I might take it into my head to reveal my identity, and become an active partner in the concern.

Even to such extremes did my imagination carry me before I reached home. But I was clear in my mind about one thing. I meant to present myself at the office in the morning, and if the chance were given me, to apprentice myself for a while. It was indeed a strange freak of destiny, that he should have been confronted by me with the same appeal that I had heard him make so short a time ago. Perhaps it were better called a strange freak of my caprice, for though of course my position was not premeditated, the words that I said to him were necessarily suggested by the analogy of the situation. I felt therefore an obligation to let his humanity work itself out, — which gave comfort and encouragement to my quixotism.

The only obstacles of serious importance to this step would be the difficulty of disposing of Aunt Helen, and as a corollary thereto the necessity of some slight deceit on my part to account for my continuance in New York. But having gone so far in the matter, I did not suffer myself to be deterred by trifles. I had, in speaking of our return to Aunt Helen this morning, dwelt on the importance of not leaving certain domestic affairs longer unattended to; and it now occurred to me to compromise with her by suggesting that she should go home, and leave me with my maid in our lodgings, which were well known to her as thoroughly quiet and respectable. As was perhaps to be expected, she resisted this proposal energetically; but as I was resolved to get rid of her at any cost, I took an obstinate stand, against which tears and flattery were equally unavailing. I made her return a condition of my remaining; otherwise I should leave the Honorable Ernest to the mercy of the maidens of New York. She must take her choice. If she decided to stay I should go home; and the only possible chance of my becoming Duchess of Clyde rested on her going home without me. The alternative was too dreadful for her to withstand my pertinacity. She wished me to remain, and rather than have her matrimonial project blocked she preferred to yield, though it was not until she had made a last appeal on the score of the extreme impropriety of my continuing to stay in New York alone.

When she had finally consented to take her departure, I wrote a note to the Honorable Ernest and to one or two other friends, announcing that we had suddenly been called home, and then I sat up far into the night putting my new-fangled wardrobe into a plausible condition. To be patched but neat seemed to me the most endurable and ingratiating, and at the same time an equally secure guise in which to figure, and I devoted my energies to accomplishing that result before morning. On that same day also, to my great relief, I succeeded in bundling off Aunt Helen without further ado, and the field was cleared for operations. I should have to trust my maid to some extent, and possibly to change my lodgings; but otherwise I had swept away all obstacles to the indulgence of this new piece of eccentricity.

It occurred to me, on the way down-town, that Mr. Prime would doubtless make some inquiries as to my previous history and present circumstances, and that I must go a step further and concoct some rational story in order to carry out my deception successfully. I was correct in my surmise. He received me with kindness, and showing me into his private office asked a few direct questions, which I answered to his satisfaction seemingly. I represented myself as one of that much-to-be pitied class, referred to by Mr. Chelm, of well-educated but impecunious young people, who only needed employment to be comfortable and happy. I had no parents, nor brothers and sisters, and up to this time had supported myself by teaching and by copying; but the stress of the times had little by little cut off the sources of my income, and when he met me yesterday I had sunk down exhausted and in despair over the prospect of finding anything to do. Such was my pitiful tale.

Fortunately my handwriting did not require to be explained away or disguised like the rest of me. It spoke for itself, being legible and bold, somewhat resembling a man's in the latter particular. Mr. Prime looked pleased as he glanced at the specimen I prepared for his inspection, and I felt that the battle was won. A few minutes later I was engaged as a confidential clerk at a modest salary. My duties for the time were to answer letters, and to copy out and arrange sets of figures at his direction; and he suggested that I should as soon as possible learn short-hand.

I could scarcely help laughing aloud as I sat and tried to realize my new position. Mr. Prime's business was as yet, I soon perceived, lamentably small. The office was commodious, but my employer had besides me only a book-keeper to help him,— a gaunt, withered-looking man of sixty. This personage glanced at me now and again over his spectacles suspiciously, and would, I dare say, have joined hands with my enemy the police officer, as to the probabilities affecting my moral character. Everything else was done by Mr. Prime, who I was pleased to notice was as spruce as ever in his personal appearance. His gloves, his boots, his cravats, and Ike, the beautifully ugly Ike, were as irreproachable as ever.

It is wonderful how easily one grows accustomed to almost any change of circumstances. Of course the first few days of my new life were excessively strange, and I passed through various stages of alarm and mortification at my own hardihood in entering upon it. But after the first week I settled down to my work with interest and composure, no longer disturbed by a fear of detection. For so skilful was my disguise that during that time I ran the gantlet of the glances both of Roger Dale and the Honorable Ernest, without exciting the suspicions of either. I am not sure that the former did not feel as if he had seen my face before, for he stared at me wonderingly, as it seemed to me, and for a moment I feared that all was over; but he turned carelessly away, and observed to my employer, loud enough for his words to reach my ears, —

" Nice looking girl that, Prime. If you don't look out, I 'll offer her double the salary across the street."

This observation directed all eyes to me, for there were several men in the group, and among them my English admirer; but in his case, at least, the adage regarding the blindness of Cupid was strikingly illustrated, for though he examined me through his lorgnette with evident admiration, he contented himself with echoing the sentiments of his financial guide, only a little more euphemistically : —

" She 's a daisy, Prime, a daisy. Reminds me too of some girl I 've seen somewhere. I 've travelled so much, and seen so many girls, I 'm always noticing likenesses. Jolly expression that,

'She's a daisy.' Only heard it yesterday; but I'm 'catching on' fast. How's Denver to-day?"

The Honorable Ernest seemed in truth to be "catching on" fast. From the remarks that were let fall by persons in the office, I judged that he must have made a great deal of money already under the tuition of Roger Dale. The success of the latter was on every one's lips. He was coining thousands daily, and was as shrewd as he was successful, according to the verdict of those whose sayings I overheard. He was not very often in our office, and I was glad to see that no intimacy existed between him and Mr. Prime. Hints dropped in my presence by some of our less flighty looking customers revealed to me the fact that there were those who predicted for him a fall as rapid as had been his rise. But I could not help feeling a little of my former jealousy return, as I noted how slack and unprofitable our business was compared with his.

I tried my best to make myself of use; and my efforts were quickly appreciated, for new and more important work was intrusted to me, under the pressure of which I felt at first completely tired out at night, and thankful to get to bed. As regards my domestic arrangements,

I decided finally not to change my lodgings, but by dint of explicit instructions to my landlady and maid, I managed to have my presence in the house concealed from those of my acquaintances who called. There are always a certain number of people who do not hear one is in town until after one has left. It was against such that I needed to take precautions; and after the impression was duly established that I was really gone, I breathed freely once more, and gave myself up to my business with little concern as to the discovery of my innocent deceit. I had to frame such replies to Aunt Helen's letters and questions as the sensitiveness of my conscience would permit.

Mr. Prime, in his effort to build up his business, was evidently most diligent and painstaking, and, as I had observed during my early investigations, usually stayed at the office until late. Of course I never left before him, and perhaps it was not unnatural that after a time we got into the way of walking up-town together. One day he happened to come back for something just as I was setting out, and he walked along by my side. Our ways lay in the same direction, and it was the habit of each of us to walk home for the sake of the exercise. It seemed to me in no way dangerous or unfitting that I should be otherwise than at ease in my conversation with Mr. Prime; indeed, I was soon conscious of a desire to mystify him by giving him a glimpse of my acquirements. I branched off from the current events of the day to poetry and art, and to my gratification I found that I had touched a sympathetic chord in my companion, which not even wonder could restrain from responding. After this it became Mr. Prime's wont to wait for me occasionally, and by the time I had been in his employ six weeks, this became his daily practice. Our intimacy was a curious one, for of course we avoided all personal and social topics, — I from necessity, and he doubtless because of the difference in our positions which he supposed to exist. But on this very account I got a truer impression of his real self, for he did not feel the hamper of conventions in our talk, and hence was not affected. He said freely what he thought and believed; and underneath the tendency to regard everything in a mezzo-cynical, mezzo-humorous light there cropped out from time to time evidences of his earnestness and enthusiasm, which as our friendship strengthened were less and less subordinated to raillery and chaff. Not a whit inferior in cultivation to myself, he possessed besides a keen analytic sense which I envied, especially as I felt that it did not steel him against ideal considerations.

Meanwhile my usefulness at the office was constantly increasing; for my employer now made me devote my time to various sorts of financial matters, and I could see plainly that he was puzzled at my aptness. He expressed the belief that I must have had experience elsewhere, for I acted, he said, as if I had been accustomed to handle large sums all my life. He offered presently to raise my salary, but I declared that what I received was sufficient for my needs. Much of the time I could see that Mr. Prime was worried, for business though active was in an unsettled state, and I knew from the books that already his capital was somewhat impaired. As I have mentioned, he was studiously devoted to his work, and the only recreation he allowed himself was his daily walk with me. I often heard Mr. Slayback, our book-keeper, into whose good graces I managed to ingratiate myself at the end of a fortnight, sigh over the unremitting industry of our employer, and declare that he would break down in health before a twelve-month was past.

"He will succeed first, and then he can afford to be an invalid," I answered; but acting on the old man's solicitude, I did all I could to lighten the load.

One afternoon, as we were walking home, I noticed that Mr. Prime seemed especially grave and moody, and I ventured to inquire if anything serious had happened.

"Oh, no; a mere trifling loss, that is unimportant in itself, but serves to impress upon me still more deeply how easy it is to imagine and difficult to perform," he answered. "It seems the simplest thing in the world to make a fortune honestly, until one attempts it."

"But why are you so anxious to make a fortune?" I asked after a silence.

"Anxious to make a fortune? Because it is my ambition; because I have always had the desire to try and spend a fortune well. Money is the greatest power in the world, and every man who is strong and vital seeks to acquire it. Why did you ask?"

"I have sometimes thought that a large fortune would be an unwelcome responsibility," I said, noticing how much his words resembled what my father had said to me. "It would be so puzzling, I should think, to spend it wisely."

"And for that reason, would you have men afraid to try? How else is the world to progress? Those who have leisure to think, are those to set mankind an example," he replied, with a fierceness that made his face glow.

My own heart welled to my lips at my companion's fervor. He however, ashamed as it were at the extravagance into which he had been betrayed, turned the conversation with some careless jest, and for the rest of the afternoon talked a badinage that did not deceive me.

"At least, let me say that I am very sorry you are worried," I added.

In the indulgence of his subsequent gayety, I noticed that Mr. Prime seemed to play the dandy more consummately than usual, as though he were reflecting that come what might he would go down as he had declared, with a smile on his face and a flawless coat on his back. I had never known him to be more amusing and nonchalant than in the half hour which followed his previous outburst. When we reached a flower-stand at the corner of the streets where our ways divided, he asked me to wait a minute, and, selecting a boutonière and a beautiful white rose, he presented the latter to me.

"You have saved me from much weariness during the past two months, Miss Bailey," he said. "This flower may brighten the dinginess of your lodgings."

Alice Bailey was the name by which I was known to Mr. Prime. I was free to take his words in any sense I chose, and believe that they had reference to my work at the office or to my companionship, or to both. In acknowledgment of his politeness I dropped a little curtsy, as I might have done to any one of my real acquaintances on a similar occasion; and as I did so, I noticed that he regarded me with a strange look of admiration.

"You did that," said he, "as if you had never done anything else; and yet, I dare say you were never in a ball-room in your life."

"Never," I answered with a smile.

"Adaptiveness, that is the word. Our people are so adaptive. But there is something about you that puzzles me more every day, Miss Bailey. Excuse my detaining you, but I am in a philosophical vein for the moment and need an audience. I would walk home with you, but you have always forbidden me that pleasure. Frankly, you have puzzled me; and that curtsy caps the climax. There are certain things adaptiveness cannot accomplish, and that is one of them."

"Have you no faith in the child of Nature?" I asked archly.

"I had none in that sense a few moments ago, but all my theories are falling to the ground. Forbear though, Miss Bailey," he said with a sudden air of sportive mystery, "you cannot afford to ruin your chances of success for the sake of a merely ornamental gift. You play the *grande dame* so well, that you are sure to reap the penalty of it. Forbear, I warn you, before it is too late. I know of what I speak. I have been a gentleman for years, and I am acquainted with all the ins and outs of the calling. It is a poor one; avoid it. But you will pardon this somewhat lengthy monologue. I have kept you from your supper. Good-night. Come, Ike."

As I tripped across the street, with all the grace and elegance at my command, I could not resist the temptation to look once over my shoulder. Mr. Prime stood watching me just where I had left him, and he raised his hat as he caught my eye, with the style of a cavalier saluting his mistress. A pretty way forsooth, thought I, for an aristocratic banker to part from his hired clerk! But I felt sure that my secret was safe.

Our relations were from this day on a different footing, or rather it was apparent to me that Mr. Prime was very partial to my society. I remember that he asked me to walk with him on the following Sunday, and we spent the beautiful spring morning in sauntering about the Park. I felt a little sorry for my companion that I should have to appear so unfashionably attired, but I did not dare to do otherwise. He seemed wholly indifferent to the circumstance, however, and I think the hours flew by too quickly for us both. I ascribed my own sensations of happiness to the loveliness of the weather.

So too it became of frequent occurrence for Mr. Prime to bring me flowers or books, and our Sunday stroll was repeated again and again. As the weather grew more balmy we substituted for it expeditions to the various resorts in the environs of the city, where we could catch a whiff of the ocean breeze, or refresh our eyes with a glimpse of the green country. These days were so pleasant to me that I avoided thinking what was to be the outcome of them. They could not last forever. Already

Aunt Helen's letters expressed an alarm at my long absence, which I was only too well aware I should soon find it impossible to allay. My salvation was the fact that she believed Mr. Ferroll to be still in town: I had failed to tell her of his departure for the West about ten days after she left. To my letters to her, which were necessarily laconic, I appended as an invariable postscript, "Not yet," by which she would understand that he had not yet put the decisive question; and sometimes when I feared lest her patience might be exhausted, I would add, "but I have hopes," which was sure to reconcile her for the time being to my staying away a little longer. To be sure I was my own mistress, but I was well aware, notwithstanding, that Aunt Helen was fully capable of coming on some fine day, with horse, foot, and dragoons, and putting a summary end to my financial idyl.

I began also to put the question to myself, why I wished to remain in New York. I had accomplished all that was possible, without revealing my identity, in the way of supervising the affairs of Francis Prime and Company. It was clearer to me than ever that a fortune could only be made by slow degrees, and that years must elapse doubtless before my protégé would attain his ambition. The letters forwarded by Mr. Chelm, and my own observations on the spot, told me that the affairs of the firm were only moderately prosperous. Especially was I convinced of the truth of this last statement, from the fact that my employer had of late mixed himself up in certain speculatious with Mr. Dale, from which he had made profits sufficient to recoup his previous losses and still show a balance in his favor. But I knew that he, as well as I, mistrusted the soundness of the firm across the street, and felt that in yielding to the temptation of following its lead he was running the risk of serious losses. Mr. Prime confessed as much to me, and declared that after a single venture to which he had already committed himself was terminated, he intended to have no more transactions with Roger Dale.

It was indeed difficult to say why I still continued to remain in Mr. Prime's employ. Although, as I have indicated, I put the question to myself sometimes, I shrank from doing so, and felt disposed to let the future take care of itself, provided I was permitted to enjoy the present undisturbed. But this was beginning to be more and more difficult. There were interests at home which could not be longer neglected without my incurring blame. I belonged to societies and clubs at which my presence was required. Then, too, it would not be many weeks before the Honorable Ernest would return to pay his promised visit to Aunt Agnes, and I felt far from sure that I should not make a mistake to discourage his advances. There was a wide difference between the sphere of an Alice Bailey and the Duchess of Clyde.

But still I delayed my return. How well I recall one Saturday afternoon in June, when as by a common instinct business men seemed to close their doors earlier than usual, and Mr. Prime and I set off to enjoy a half holiday in our usual fashion. He was at the height of good spirits, for the affair in which he was interested jointly with Roger Dale was doing wonderfully well, and the profits promised to be enormous. Absorbed in conversation, we failed to notice the close proximity of a rapidly driven horse, from under the hoofs of which I escaped by a mere hair's breadth. It was a trivial incident in itself, but the exclamation which my companion made, and the eager impetuous way in which he expressed himself regarding my safety, served to open my eyes to the real condition of affairs between us. There was no use in my seeking longer to conceal from myself the reason for my remaining in New York. It was Mr. Prime's society that held me there, and decency bade me to put an end to our relations at once, but on his account far more than on my own; for while I flattered myself that my heart was untouched save by the emotion of a warm friendship, I could not dismiss the conviction that his feeling for me was rapidly approaching the point at which friendship becomes an impossibility. I must go, and immediately. It was foolish and culpable of me to have stayed so long. A girl in the first blush of maidenhood might excuse herself on the score of not recognizing the signs of a more than Platonic interest, but for me such an apology could not be other than a subterfuge. Mr. Prime had worry enough already, and why add to it the pain of an unrequited attachment? I would go on Monday. To-morrow we were to walk once more, and I would frame some excuse, which he would never suspect, for severing our connections.

But parallel with these reflections was a certain element of curiosity in my mind as to whether Francis Prime would be ever so far carried away by his liking for me as to ask me to become his wife,— me, Alice Bailey, his poor, hired clerk! I wondered that I should be especially interested in the matter, for its ludicrous side was at once apparent; that is to say, the situations portrayed in cheap contemporaneous fiction, of beautiful working-girls led to the altar by the sons of rich bankers, immediately suggested themselves. But nevertheless the thought haunted me, and I did not feel altogether the degree of contrition at the idea of having captivated him that I perhaps should have done. If it was not for myself alone that he loved me, what was his love worth? If the lowliness of my position deterred him from asking me to marry him, I was wasting sympathy upon him, and taking needless precautions. The idea roused me strangely, and I found myself taking sides against myself in an imaginary debate as to the probabilities of his conduct. It made every vein in my body tingle, to think that birth or fortune might be able to affect his decision; and it seemed to me, as I sought my pillow that night, that I almost hated him.

In the morning I decided that I had probably overestimated his feelings toward me, and that although I had better go home on the following day, there was no reason why I should treat Mr. Prime other than as usual. He was not in love with me; or if he were, he was not man enough to acknowledge it. I should refuse him if he did; but I hated to feel that I had been expending so much friendship on a man whose soul could not soar beyond birth and fortune. Had he not told me that money was the greatest power on earth? So, too, he had said to my face that a lady could not be made, but was born. I was irrational, and I was conscious of being irrational; but I did not care. I would make him wince at least, and feel for a time the tortures of a love he did not dare to express. Ah! but such a love was not worthy of the name, and it was I who was become the fitting subject for the finger of derision, because I had put my faith in him.

These were the thoughts that harassed me before I met Mr. Prime on Sunday, and we turned our steps with tacit unanimity toward the Park. I walked in silence, chafing inwardly; and he too, I fancy, was nervous and self-absorbed, though I paid little heed to his emotions, so complex were my own. We had not proceeded very far before he turned to me and said simply,—

"What is the matter? Have I offended you in any way?"

"Do you think then, Mr. Prime, that my thoughts must always be of you?" I answered.

"Alas! no. But something has happened. You cannot deceive me."

I was silent a moment. "Yes, something has happened. I am going to leave New York."

"Going to leave New York!" he stopped abruptly, and looked at me with amazement.

"Yes," I said quietly. "My aunt has sent for me, and it is imperative that I should go. She is in trouble and needs me. It is a long story, and one with which I will not weary you. It is not necessary that you should be burdened with my private affairs; you have enough troubles of your own. Let us change the subject, please. But you will have to let me go to-morrow, Mr. Prime. I am very sorry to inconvenience you, but, as I have already said, it is imperative."

My words were so cold that I could see he was puzzled, and my heart softened toward him a little. At least he had been kind to me. He walked on for a few moments without speaking. We entered the Park, and turned into a path where we should be unobserved.

"I have no right to inquire into your private affairs, I well know," he said presently, "but I wish you would let me help you."

"I am sure of your sympathy, Mr. Prime; and if you could be of any service in the matter, I would call upon you."

"Where does your aunt live?"

"I had rather not answer that question."

He looked grave, and as I glanced at him a frown passed over his face. "He is thinking doubtless," thought I, "that it is I who have done something wrong, and am trying to mislead him; or he is reflecting how wise he was not to offer himself to a woman with whose antecedents he is unacquainted. He mistrusts me at the first hint of suspicion, and would sacrifice his love on the altar of conventionality." Curiously enough, I seemed to take it for granted that he was in love with me.

"And you must go to-morrow?" he asked.

"To-morrow, without fail."

"But you will return soon?"

"I do not expect to return at all."

"Impossible! You cannot go!" he said with a sudden outburst; but he corrected himself in a restrained voice: "I do not mean, of course, that you cannot go if you choose."

"I am quite aware, Mr. Prime, that this will cause you great annoyance," said I. "If it were possible for me to remain until you could find another assistant without neglecting duties that are still more important, I would do so."

He made a motion as though to wave that consideration aside. "No one can take your place. But that is not all. Let us sit down, Miss Bailey; I have something to say to you. I had meant to say it very soon, but it must be said now or never. I love you!"

I trembled like a leaf at his avowal, — I did not even yet know why.

"I love you from the bottom of my soul," he said once more, and now his words were poured out in a passionate flood, to which I listened with a strange joy that thrilled me through and through.

"I have never loved before. You are the first, the very first woman in the world who has ever touched my heart. I did not know what it was to love until a few days ago, and I could not understand how friendship should seem so sweet. But last night, when I saw you almost trampled under foot and swept away forever from me, I knew that what I had begun to guess, was the truth."

"It is impossible for you to love me. I am merely a poor friendless girl, without fortune or position," I murmured.

"Yes, yes, you are; and that is the strange and wonderful part of it all. I love and adore you, in spite of theory and principle and the judgment of wise men. But I defy their laughter and their sneers, for I can point to you and say, 'Show me her match among the daughters of the proud and wealthy. She is the peer of any.' I disbelieved in the power of Nature to imitate the excellence of woman, and I am punished for my lack of faith. And how sweet and exquisite the punishment, if only, Alice, you will tell me that my prayer is granted, and that you will be my wife."

"Ah! but I should only be a burden to you. I can bring you nothing, not even an untarnished name, for though you see me as I am, you do not know what others whose blood is in my veins have done."

"What is that to me?" he cried fiercely; "it is you that I love!"

"But you are striving to become rich. It is your ambition. Have you not told me so? Money is the greatest power on earth. You said that, too."

"And it was a lie. I had never loved. What is money to me now? But, no, I am wrong. It *is* my ambition, and without your sympathy and affection I shall never attain it."

He gazed at me imploringly, and yet though my eyes were overflowing with tears in the fulness of my new-found happiness, I still shook my head.

"Listen to me, Mr. Prime," I said quietly, after a short silence between us. "I am very grateful to you — how could I be otherwise? — for what you have said to me. Yours were the sweetest and most precious words to which I ever listened. You have asked me to become your wife, because you loved me for myself alone: that I can be sure of, since I have nothing but myself to bring you. It makes me more happy than I dare think of; but in spite of all you have said to me, I cannot accept your sacrifice. I cannot consent to mar your hopes for the future with all I lack. You think you love me now, and I believe you; but the time might come when you would see that you had made a mistake, and that would kill me. I am not of your opinion as to the power of Nature to imitate the excellence of woman. You were right at first. Ladies are born, not made; and were you to marry in the station of life in which you see me, the scales would some day drop from your eyes, and you would know that you had been deceived by love. No, Mr. Prime, I should not be worthy to become your wife were I to accept your offer. The difference between us is too great, and the banker and his hired female clerk will never be on an equality to the end of the world. I am sorry — ah, so sorry! — to wound you thus, but I cannot permit you to throw your life away."

"Then you do not love me?" he asked, with a piteous cry.

"Love you?" I gave a little joyous laugh before I said, "I shall never love any one else in the world."

It would take too long to repeat the efforts Mr. Prime made to lead me to reconsider my resolution. Meanwhile I was racking my brains to find a way of letting matters rest without depriving him utterly of hope. As he said, the knowledge that my heart was his only increased the bitterness of his despair. Happy as I was, I felt bewildered and uncertain. I shrank instinctively from revealing my identity at once. I wanted time to think. I scarcely knew the character of my own emotions. At one moment I blushed with a sense of the web of deceit that I had wound about him, and at another with the joyful consciousness of our mutual love. What would he say when the truth was made known to him? Ah! but he loves me for myself alone, was the answering thought.

I had continued to shake my head as the sole response to his burning petition; but at last I turned to him and said that if he were content to wait, say a year, and let his passion have time to cool, I might be less obdurate. But in the interim he was to make no effort to discover my whereabouts, or to follow me. He must not even write to me (perhaps I had a secret idea that too many letters strangle love), but pursue the tenor of his way as though I had never existed. If at the end of that time he still wished me to become his wife, it might be I should no longer refuse. It was better for us both, I said, that we should part for the present. He must consider himself free as air, and I should think him sensible if on reflection he strove to banish me from his thoughts.

"A year is a long time," he answered.

"Long enough, almost, to make a fortune in, as well as to become wise and prudent."

By making him wait, I should let the banking-scheme develop itself a little further.

When by dint of my refusal to yield further he was forced to consent to these terms, we gave ourselves up to enjoyment of the few hours which we could still pass together. I talked and laughed, over-bubbling with happiness; but he would sigh ever and anon, as though he felt that I were about to slip from his sight to return no more. Once in the gayety of my mood I called Ike to me, and stooped to pat his pudgy sides. "Ike the imperious, beautifully ugly Ike!" I cried with glee, and with a daring that but for its very boldness might have disclosed all.

But my lover was in no mood to make deductions. "You seem so joyous, Alice, one would suppose that you were glad to leave me."

"I am joyous, — yes, very joyous, — for I have been brave enough to save the man I love from a *mésalliance.*"

V.

THE effect on a woman of the revelation that she loves him who has proffered her his heart, is like the awakening of buds in spring, which beneath the soft mysterious breath of an invisible power burst their bonds with graceful reluctance, and shyly gladden Nature.

It seemed to me as if I had never lived before. Unlike the untutored passion of my extreme youth, my happiness was calm and reflective, but none the less satisfying. Under its sway I found it a comparatively easy task to overcome the querulousness and revive the hopes of Aunt Helen on my return home. It was my desire, of course, to avoid any further deception, and I sought refuge in silence, beyond the statement that the future Duke of Clyde had gone to the West without making any definite proposal. But I assured her that he was certain to visit us within a few months.

I took up the round of my avocations as if nothing had happened. We had hired a cottage at Newport for the summer, and there I ensconced myself, and strove by means of books and friends to keep the alternate exuberance and depression of my spirits within bounds. But though I was at times melancholy for a sight of my lover, joy was chiefly predominant in my heart, — so much so that people commented on my cheerfulness, and Aunt Helen dropped occasional hints which led me to believe she cherished secretly the opinion that I was enamoured of her idol.

My visits to Mr. Chelm's office were of course renewed. I told him that I had visited the street where the office of Francis Prime and Company was situated, and had been pleased at getting a glimpse of it. In answer to my questions as to what he thought of the progress of the firm he said very little, except that all business was in an unsettled state, owing to the speculative spirit that had followed the long period of stagnation. As yet, my protégé seemed to have been generally prudent, but it needed the experience of a tried business man to resist the temptations to make money by short cuts presented at the present time. He judged from the last report sent him, that he had been lately making one or two successful ventures in a doubtful class of securities, and he should take it upon himself, with my permission, to give him advice to avoid them for the future.

I felt an eager desire to say he had already promised that the speculation in which he was now engaged should be the last; but that of course was impossible, without disclosing my secret. How should I ever have the face to make confession to Mr. Chelm when the time came, if it ever did come?

As the months slipped away, I began to be haunted occasionally by the thought that a year was a longer time than I had supposed, and it might be that Francis Prime would take me at my word, and try to forget me. At such moments my heart seemed to stand still, and a weary vista of monotonous and never-ceasing maidenhood arose before me. It would be preferable to die than to be deceived now. I would not doubt; and indeed I did not doubt. But who can control the changing moods of the imagination?

I think the consciousness that such a thing as his proving false was a possibility affected my treatment of my maiden aunts, and made me more gentle and considerate in regard to their foibles. The early lives of both of them were sealed books to me, excepting the glimpse Aunt Helen had given me of hers at the time of my own first sorrow. Who could tell that there was not in their hearts some bit of cruel treachery or misunderstanding still remembered though unmentioned, which had seared and withered existence for them? It was this feeling among others, that urged me to write to Aunt Agnes and ask permission to spend a day or two with her before we finally returned to town. She never left the city, preferring, as she declared, the stability of the bricks and mortar, to being drowned at the sea-side or mangled by cattle in the country. Rather to my surprise, she said in her answer that she had been on the point of writing to me herself, but would now defer mentioning the matter she had in mind until we met.

As I had divined, the subject that was engrossing her as regards me was the coming visit of the Honorable Ernest Ferroll. She had heard from him at San Francisco to the effect that he was on the point of starting for the East, and that he took the liberty of forwarding to her his letters of introduction as preliminary to paying his respects to her in person. But on the particular evening of my arrival I found Aunt

Agnes oblivious to everything except a piece of information which, though far from incredible to me, had evidently been to her like lightning from a clear sky. The forbidding manner in which she received me led me to fancy that I had displeased her; and remembering her previous discovery, the awful suspicion that she had ferreted out my secret seized me for an instant. But I was speedily reassured.

"I am glad you are here, Virginia, if only to read this. You were right, child, after all; and I am an old fool, over whose eyes any one seems to be able to pull the wool."

She spoke in her sternest tones, and held out to me a newspaper in which was the announcement of the nuptials of Mr. Charles Liversage Spence and Miss Lucretia Kingsley, — "no cards."

"Did you not know they were engaged?" I inquired.

"I know nothing but what you see there," replied my aunt; "and what is more, I wish to know nothing further."

"They have acted for some time as if they were engaged. If they are in love with each other it seems best that they should be married, after all," I said, not caring to express my opinion as to the especial fitness of the match with any greater emphasis.

"In love with each other! What right had she to fall in love with him, I should like to know?" she exclaimed with indignation. "She a mere disciple, a pupil, to fall in love with the master; aspire to be the wife of a man as far superior to her as a planet to an ordinary star! Bah! Fall in love with him! Tell *me!* It was bad enough when he fell in love with you, Virginia; but this is fifty times worse, because she knew better, and understood the value of celibacy to such a life. Her conduct amounts to utter selfishness."

"I think Miss Kingsley has had designs on Mr. Spence for a long time. That was why she was so bitter against me," I said.

"Would that you had married him, Virginia! I could have endured that. But this is disgusting! I never wish to see either of them again," emphatically remarked Aunt Agnes.

It was useless to represent to her that Mrs. Spence was very much in love with her husband, and that on that account would doubtless strive to make him happy. It was the fact of their marriage that distressed her; and, unlike me, she did not think of pitying Mr. Spence because of any flaws in the disposition of his wife. I tried therefore to dismiss the matter from the conversation as soon as possible; and before the end of the evening her mood was so far mollified that she introduced the subject of the Honorable Ernest's arrival.

"Yes, Virginia," she said, "it is forty-one years ago that I made the ocean passage with that young man's father, and we have corresponded ever since. That is what comes of being systematic in one's habits. Now, don't go fancying that there was anything more in it than there really was. We were friends simply, nothing else. But a friend means something to me; and I mean to receive this young man into my house, and show him every attention in my power. And you tell me that you have met him in New York, and like him very much? I am not a match-maker, Virginia, like your Aunt Helen; but it would doubtless be very agreeable to both the families if you young people should happen to take a fancy to each other. Stranger things have occurred; and since it is evident to me from an intimate knowledge of your character that you are sure to marry some day, I know of no one whom it would please me so much to intrust your future happiness to, as the son of my old friend. His presumptive rank would probably weigh for more with you than with me. Provided the young man has high principles and a steadfast purpose, I shall be content."

I laughed gently in reply. I had made up my mind not to thwart the old lady openly. It would be time enough for that later, if the Honorable Britain ever should come to the point. It was such a novel coincidence that my aunts should agree for once on anything, that the thought of putting myself in antagonism with them did not occur to me seriously for a moment. I felt the humor of the situation, and was also filled at once with the desire to harmonize them forever by means of this common interest.

"We will see, Aunt Agnes, what he thinks of me," I said; and all through my visit of two days I dropped hints of the efforts Aunt Helen had made in New York to prejudice Mr. Ferroll in my favor.

"She has spoiled all, I dare say, by showing her hand too openly," bristled Aunt Agnes, the first time I mentioned the subject.

"In that case, you will have to let him have a glimpse of the Harlan pride," I answered. "I shall depend on you not to allow me to be forced upon him, Aunt Agnes. I am sure, however, that Aunt Helen means well in the matter. She may be a little indiscreet, but if you were to talk it over with her I am sure you would come to a satisfactory agreement. Now, it strikes me as an excellent idea for you to come and spend a few days with us at Newport. It would give us both very great pleasure. Please do think of it seriously."

"Newport? Do you take me for a fashionable do-nothing, child? Why, your aunt would n't let me inside the door! I have only six dresses in the world. Newport! Tell *me!*"

"What nonsense, Aunt Agnes! I promise you that you shall have the warmest of welcomes if you will come, and you may, if you prefer, wear the same dress all the time you are there."

I did not press the matter at the moment, but I recurred to it many times afterwards; and as soon as I got home I told Aunt Helen of Aunt Agnes' proposal to invite Mr. Ferroll to her own house, and of her general enthusiasm in regard to his proposed visit.

"Bravo!" she responded, clapping her hands. "Your aunt shows her sense for once in her life, though one would have to be blind as a mole not to see that this is one chance in a thousand."

"What should you say to asking her down here for a few days?"

"Certainly, dear. She does n't know any one, to be sure, and would probably dress like an antediluvian. But people would n't think any thing of that, if it was whispered around that she is literary and peculiar. I think on the whole it would be a good plan to ask her. I can give her a few ideas as to how a nobleman should be handled."

"Precisely," I answered.

Accordingly, Aunt Helen and I each wrote a most urgent letter of invitation; and after some further correspondence, my efforts were rewarded with the presence in my house of my father's sister. For the first twenty-four hours, despite my cordial welcome, I feared every moment lest she should announce her intention of going home again. Her manner was so stiff, and Aunt Helen's so airy, that I was apprehensive of a catastrophe. But at last by the display of tact, and by carefully humoring their respective prejudices, I drew them gradually together; and when at last I was taken apart by each of them successively one evening, to be told that save for certain unfortunate peculiarities her rival was an uncommonly sensible woman, I felt that

I could safely retire, and leave them to their day-dream of making me Duchess of Clyde.

"Duchess or no duchess, it would be an admirable connection," said Aunt Agnes.

"And there is no shadow of a doubt that his wife will be a duchess," added Aunt Helen.

One day, shortly after we had returned to town, the news reached us that the Honorable Ernest Ferroll was in New York, and as a consequence there was great excitement among those who had been told of his projected visit to our city. In her wish to make the young nobleman comfortable, Aunt Agnes had yielded to the remonstrances of her former enemy as to the necessity of renovating her house, and accordingly was absorbed by plumbers, upholsterers, and decorators, who under the general supervision of Aunt Helen undermined the customs of a lifetime, but cemented this new friendship. The last touches were being put to the improvements, and complete harmony reigned between the two establishments. To think of Aunt Agnes dropping in on Aunt Helen, or Aunt Helen drinking tea with Aunt Agnes!

It therefore happened that I was taken very little notice of by my two relatives, and was free to indulge the sweet current of sentiment, of which they were so blissfully unaware, to my heart's content. The power of love, and the power of money! How when united did they each illumine the other, — they, the two greatest forces of the world!

On the morning following the day on which we heard of Mr. Ferroll's arrival in New York, I saw a statement in the daily paper which made me start violently. It was the announcement of the failure of Roger Dale, banker and broker, with liabilities of three millions and estimated assets of less than one hundred thousand. I hastened to get ready to call on Mr. Chelm, but before leaving the house I received a message from him which read as follows: "Francis Prime is in town, and I have made an appointment with him for twelve o'clock. You will please come to the office at once, if possible."

"What has happened, Mr. Chelm?" I asked, as I entered the room where he was sitting. I tried to seem calm and indifferent.

"Sit down, Miss Harlan. I am sorry to say that your friend Francis Prime has got into difficulties. Roger Dale, a rather prominent banker, has suspended payment, and Mr. Prime happens to be one of his largest creditors."

"Has Mr. Prime failed also?"

"Not yet. But I see no escape for him on his own showing. The circumstances are peculiar, and indicate deliberate fraud on the part of Dale; but, as Prime says, he can't let his own customers suffer."

"This is all a riddle to me," I said, a little impatiently. "You forget that I do not know the facts yet."

"The facts are simple enough; and the whole difficulty, it seems, is indirectly the result of having anything to do with men who take improper risks. As I told you the other day, young Prime has been egged on by the large sums he has seen made in a few days by others, to go joint account with this man Dale, who has had the reputation of being very shrewd and successful, and who, by the way, comes from this city. The speculations turned out very well, especially this last one, which our friend tells me was to have been his last."

"Yes, I am sure it was," I answered excitedly.

Mr. Chelm looked at me with a blank sort of gaze. "Very likely," he observed, with a dry smile. "Well, as I was saying, this like the others was profitable, and Prime not only had enriched himself but some of his customers who had taken the risk with him. The money was paid to him, and he made reports of the same to his customers. But the same day Dale came in and asked Prime to loan him over night the sum he had just paid in, as a personal favor. Prime says he hesitated, not because he suspected anything, but on grounds of common prudence. It seemed to him, however, that it would be churlish and punctilious to refuse to accommodate the man to whom he owed his good fortune, and so he lent the money. Next day, Dale failed disgracefully. Of course Mr. Prime feels bound in honor to pay his customers their profits, which happen to exceed his capital. There is the whole story."

"I see. And what do you advise me to do?" I asked, after a pause.

"Do?" Mr. Chelm shrugged his shoulders. "I do not see that you can do anything."

"I can pay his debts."

"You can pay his debts, and you can found a Home for unsuccessful merchant-princes, if you choose, but not with my consent."

"He has behaved very honorably."

"Pooh! Any honest man would do the same."

"You say he will be here at twelve?"

"At twelve."

"Why did you ask him to come back?"

"You interrogate like a lawyer. I told him I would communicate with my principal."

"Did he ask for help?"

"Not at all. He was ready to 'stand the racket,' he said. He merely wished to state the facts. He blamed himself for lack of discretion, and I could not contradict him. He was immaculate as ever in his personal appearance, but he looked pale."

"Poor fellow!"

"Yes, it is unfortunate, I admit. But it will teach him a lesson. A man who wishes to become a merchant-prince cannot afford to trust anybody."

"What a doctrine!"

"Business and sentiment are incompatible."

I was silent a moment. "Mr. Chelm, when he comes here at twelve, I want you to tell him that he shall not fail, and that I will pay his debts."

"Miss Harlan, do not be so foolish, I beseech you!"

"But I will do this only on one condition, and that is, — that he will marry me."

"What!"

I blushed before the lawyer's gaze and exclamation.

"Marry you?"

"Yes, Mr. Chelm. Do not be too much surprised. Trust me. I know what I am doing, believe me. Have I not hitherto usually been moderately sensible?"

"Up to this time I have regarded you as an uncommonly wise young woman; but this is sheer madness."

"As you please. But you will comply with my request if I insist?"

"He will accept the offer."

"If he does, you are to give me away, you remember. But I am sure he will not accept."

"You were sure he would make a fortune."

"But it was you who put the idea of marrying him into my head."

"I am to be made to bear the blame, of course. There is one hope, however, — he thinks you sixty-five."

"Ah! but he must be undeceived. You must tell him I am young and very beautiful."

"What madness is this, Virginia?"

"Trust me, Mr. Chelm, and do what I ask you."

"Very well."

"You will tell him?"

"If you insist."

"And I shall be in the other room and overhear it all. Stop, one thing more. In case he refuses, make him promise to come to see me this afternoon for a half hour. That at least he will not have the discourtesy to deny me. But only if he refuses, mind."

"Do you really wish me to make this offer?" said Mr. Chelm, as a last appeal.

"I was never more in earnest in my life," I replied.

A half hour later, Mr. Prime entered, followed as usual by Ike. I had made Mr. Chelm promise that he would leave no argument unused to induce Francis to accept my offer. He looked pale and worn, but there was nothing despairing or otherwise than manly in his air.

"I have seen my principal, sir," said Mr. Chelm with abruptness. "She is very sorry for you."

"I thank her with all my heart. And some day I hope to be able to restore to her the money which I have lost through my credulity."

"It is of that I wish to speak. Please sit

down. My client does not wish you to fail. She will pay your debts."

" Impossible ! "

" Please do not interrupt me. But she demands of you a favor in return."

" It is her's to command, whatever it is; but I will take no more money."

" Wait until you hear what I have to say. In consideration of what she has done for you, and what she is ready to do for you, she asks you to become her husband."

" Her husband ? "

" Yes, that is the favor."

Francis Prime stood confounded, as if he were doubting either his sanity or that of his companion.

" Her husband ? Wishes me to become her husband ? "

" Why not ? She loves you."

" She is an old lady, you told me."

" Did I ? I was trying to conceal from you then that she is young and excessively beautiful. I will tell you more. She is worth four millions in her own right."

" What is her name ? "

" That I will tell you also, — Miss Virginia Harlan."

"I have heard of her. And she loves me?"

"Desperately. Come, sir, you hesitate, it seems to me. This is a chance that does not come every day."

"Heavens and earth, what am I to say?"

"Say you accept. You asked my advice once, and now I give it to you again."

"But I do not love her."

"A mere bagatelle. You would very soon."

"I am of another opinion. I could never love her, for the reason," — he paused an instant, — "for the reason that I love some one else."

"Ah! if you are married, that settles it."

"I am not married."

"Young man, you are a great fool then." The lawyer was really waxing angry. "This young lady is the superior of any man I know. You are throwing away a prize."

"That may be, sir. But if you recall a speech I made in this office some six months ago, you will remember that I said I was a gentleman. If I should accept the offer you make me, I should be one no longer. And I prize my reputation in that respect more than I cherish anything in the world."

"This sounds well, sir, but it is childishness. You are bound to make my client amends for your folly. It is in your power to marry her, and if you are a man you will make her that reparation."

"Excuse me, Mr. Chelm, it would be foolish for us to argue longer on this point. I will call again to-morrow, when we are both less excited. Do not think I wish time to reflect, for my decision is final. But I should like your client to know that I am not wholly an ingrate. To-morrow, if you say so, at the same hour."

"Stop one moment. I have one more request to make of you, which you can hardly refuse, perverse as you seem to be. My client expressed the wish that in case you should decide as you have done, you would call upon her this evening at her own house."

Francis bit his lip. "I should be obliged to make the same answer."

"The subject, sir, will not be broached."

"Certainly, then, I will come."

It was with difficulty that I could restrain myself from rushing into the room and falling at his feet; but when I knew that he was gone, I went up to Mr. Chelm with the tears in my eyes.

"I did my best for you, Virginia. But the fellow is right. He is a gentleman. I hated him for causing you such pain, but if he loves some one else — well — one can scarcely blame him."

"I told you he would refuse me. Do not mind my tears; and promise me that you will come to-night."

"What new mystery is this?"

"Never you mind; only promise that you will come."

How shall I describe that meeting? To begin with, I went home and broke the news to Aunt Helen and Aunt Agnes that my husband to be was to pass the evening with us, and for the moment did not break to them another bit of news I had heard before leaving Mr. Chelm,— that the Honorable Ernest Ferroll, having made a large fortune in the stock market through the agency of Mr. Dale, had withdrawn it from his hands in time, so as not to have it swallowed up by the failure, and had sailed for England. It was money he wanted, not me.

But both my aunts, poor old ladies, fancied, I fear, that it was the future Duke of Clyde who was to be the guest of the evening; and when

Francis Prime was ushered in, although he looked distinguished enough to be a Prince, Aunt Helen, at least, suspected that there was something wrong. As I afterwards learned, her air towards my lover was distant and haughty; and as Aunt Agnes had begun of late to imitate her former enemy, his reception was not cordial. But while he was looking from one to another with some hesitation, Mr. Chelm, who was standing in one corner of the room, by previous agreement pulled away the drapery that covered the portrait of me painted by Paul Barr, which stood in the middle of the room.

Francis gave a start, and flung up both his hands. "Who is that?" he cried.

"That, sir, is my niece," replied Aunt Helen with haughtiness. "Are you not acquainted with her?"

"Impossible! It is Alice Bailey."

"Yes, Francis," I said, coming into the room, "it is Alice Bailey; but it is Virginia Harlan as well. The power of love and the power of money! My own sweet husband, you are mine forever, — that is, if you will have me. Ike the imperious, beautifully ugly Ike," — for I had released the dog from the vestibule to share our happiness, — "you are mine now, as well as his."

It was thus that I gave expression to my happiness, clasped in the arms of him I loved, and who loved me, while the others were too dazed to speak. But when the time came for me to be given away, it was Mr. Chelm who said the necessary words.

In adding that my aunts never quarrelled again, I have told of my autobiography all that can possibly interest the public.

University Press: John Wilson & Son, Cambridge.

TICKNOR AND COMPANY'S
ANNOUNCEMENTS OF
NEW BOOKS
TO BE PUBLISHED DURING THE AUTUMN AND WINTER OF
1886.

The Prices named below are subject to Revision on Publication.

JUST PUBLISHED.

A ROMANTIC YOUNG LADY. By ROBERT GRANT, author of "The Confessions of a Frivolous Girl," etc. 12mo. $1.50.

 This is the latest and one of the strongest works of the successful delineator of modern society life and manners. It will be read eagerly and enjoyably by thousands of lovers of the best fiction.

 Mr. Grant's recent work, "Face to Face," has given him renewed prestige among all readers, and will insure a hearty welcome and large sale for this still later production of his genius.

Uniform with "LUCILE" *and* "THE LADY OF THE LAKE," *Two New and choice Editions of*

BYRON'S CHILDE HAROLD. Tremont Edition. 1 vol. 16mo. Beautifully Illustrated. With red lines, bevelled boards, and gilt edges, $2.50; half-calf, $4.00; tree-calf, antique morocco, flexible calf or seal, $5.00.

BYRON'S CHILDE HAROLD. Pocket Edition. 1 vol. Little-Classic size. With thirty illustrations. Elegantly bound, $1.00; half-calf, $2.25; antique morocco, flexible calf or seal, $3.00; tree-calf, or padded calf, $3.50.

 These new and beautiful editions of these perennially popular poems are made from *entirely new electrotype-plates*, in large and easily legible type, with more than thirty exquisite illustrations.

 As these are the newest, handsomest, and cheapest, they cannot fail to become the best selling editions in the market.

SHAKESPEARE'S ENGLAND. By WILLIAM WINTER. 1 vol. 24mo. flexible covers, 50 cents.

 This is a small pocket volume of 270 pages, printed at Edinburgh, in the beautiful clear typography which characterizes the work of the Edinburgh University Press. The covers are emblazoned with the Shakespeare arms and the roses of England, making a singularly attractive little book. The subject-matter is largely the same (but not including all) that appears in the same author's "The Trip to England" and "English Rambles;" and includes these chapters: The Voyage — The Beauty of England — Great Historic Places — Rambles in London — A Visit to Windsor — The Palace of Westminster — Warwick and Kenilworth — First View of Stratford-on-Avon — London Nooks and Corners — Relics of Lord Byron — Westminster Abbey — The Home of Shakespeare — Up to London — Old Churches of London — Literary Shrines of London — A Haunt of Edmund Kean — Stoke-Pogis and Thomas Gray — At the Grave of Coleridge — On Barnet Battle-field — A Glimpse of Canterbury — The Shrines of Warwickshire — A Borrower of the Night.

A List of Books Published by

THE HOLIDAY BOOK OF THE SEASON.

SCOTT'S THE LAY OF THE LAST MINSTREL. An entirely new edition of this famous and popular poem, from *new plates*, with nearly *one hundred* new illustrations by leading American artists. Elegantly and appropriately bound, with full gilt edges. In box. Cloth, $6.00; padded calf, tree-calf, or antique morocco, $10.00. A few copies in crushed Levant, with silk linings, $25.00.

"The Lay of the Last Minstrel" is larger than its predecessors, the Holiday volumes published under Mr. Anthony's supervision, and its broad and handsome pages offer very favorable opportunities for the display of the illustrations, which are masterpieces of modern engraving.

The immediate and permanent success of "The Lady of the Lake," "Marmion," etc., has encouraged the publishers to bring out this not less popular and famous poem. It is produced in the same style, and with the same careful and elaborate style of illustration, regardless of cost, while Mr. Anthony's skilful supervision is sufficient guarantee that the work is elegant and tasteful as well as correct. The publishers feel assured that the work in its new and beautiful shape will be the **Leading Holiday Book of the Year.**

THE PETERKIN PAPERS. By LUCRETIA P. HALE. New Holiday edition, revised and enlarged, uniform with "Davy and the Goblin." Square 4to. Illustrated with a great number of new pictures. $1.50.

The continued popularity of these inimitable stories has compelled the issue of this new and enlarged edition, with new illustrations and type. "The Lady from Philadelphia," "Agamemnon," "Solomon John," and other characters of these stories have become household words in thousands of American families; and the publication of a worthy and comely edition of so delightful a classic will be hailed with joy by many old friends and new.

MURAL PAINTING. By FREDERIC CROWNINSHIELD. 1 vol. Square 8vo. With numerous diagrams and full-page illustrations. $3.00.

This series of papers has excited great interest and attention in "The American Architect;" and in its present enlarged and amended form, with many new illustrations, is still more valuable.

THE VIRGINIA CAMPAIGN OF GENERAL POPE IN 1862. Being Volume II. of Papers read before the Military Historical Society of Massachusetts. With Maps and Plans. 1 vol. 8vo. $3.00.

A careful and dispassionate account of the great retreat from the Rapidan to the Potomac, with the stories of its terrible battles, prepared by prominent military officers, and dealing with the Second Bull-Run campaign, the Fitz-John Porter affair, and other interesting matters.

SONGS AND SATIRES. A volume of poems. By JAMES JEFFREY ROCHE. 1 vol. 12mo. $1.00.

The range and versatility of these poems add to their other attractions, and make the volume a very popular one. Mr. Roche's *vers de société*, printed in "Life," and other publications, are of singular delicacy and originality, and the best of them are incorporated in this volume, together with many heretofore unpublished poems.

GENIUS IN SUNSHINE AND IN SHADOW. By M. M. BALLOU, author of "Edge-tools of Speech." 1 vol. 12mo. $1.50.

Mr. Ballou has for many years been known as one of the most industrious, accurate, and entertaining of American scholars. The present volume (his latest work) is a peculiarly interesting one, full of anecdotes and *memorabilia*, which set forth the intimate inner lives of the world's heroes and notables. They have been gathered from the most recondite sources, and skilfully massed in attractive array, forming a great collection, that is at once valuable and interesting.

TICKNOR AND COMPANY'S
ANNOUNCEMENTS OF
NEW BOOKS
TO BE PUBLISHED DURING THE AUTUMN AND WINTER OF
1886.

The Prices named below are subject to Revision on Publication.

JUST PUBLISHED.

A ROMANTIC YOUNG LADY. By ROBERT GRANT, author of "The Confessions of a Frivolous Girl," etc. 12mo. $1.50.

This is the latest and one of the strongest works of the successful delineator of modern society life and manners. It will be read eagerly and enjoyably by thousands of lovers of the best fiction.

Mr. Grant's recent work, "Face to Face," has given him renewed prestige among all readers, and will insure a hearty welcome and large sale for this still later production of his genius.

Uniform with "LUCILE" and "THE LADY OF THE LAKE," Two New and choice Editions of

BYRON'S CHILDE HAROLD. Tremont Edition. 1 vol. 16mo. Beautifully illustrated. With red lines, bevelled boards, and gilt edges, $2.50; half-calf, $4.00; tree-calf, antique morocco, flexible calf or seal, $5.00.

BYRON'S CHILDE HAROLD. Pocket Edition. 1 vol. Little-Classic size. With thirty illustrations. Elegantly bound, $1.00; half-calf, $2.25; antique morocco, flexible calf or seal, $3.00; tree-calf, or padded calf, $3.50.

These new and beautiful editions of these perennially popular poems are made from *entirely new electrotype-plates*, in large and easily legible type, with more than thirty exquisite illustrations.

As these are the newest, handsomest, and cheapest, they cannot fail to become the best selling editions in the market.

SHAKESPEARE'S ENGLAND. By WILLIAM WINTER. 1 vol. 24mo. flexible covers, 50 cents.

This is a small pocket volume of 270 pages, printed at Edinburgh, in the beautiful clear typography which characterizes the work of the Edinburgh University Press. The covers are emblazoned with the Shakespeare arms and the roses of England, making a singularly attractive little book. The subject-matter is largely the same (but not including all) that appears in the same author's "The Trip to England" and "English Rambles;" and includes these chapters: The Voyage — The Beauty of England — Great Historic Places — Rambles in London — A Visit to Windsor — The Palace of Westminster — Warwick and Kenilworth — First View of Stratford-on-Avon — London Nooks and Corners — Relics of Lord Byron — Westminster Abbey — The Home of Shakespeare — Up to London — Old Churches of London — Literary Shrines of London — A Haunt of Edmund Kean — Stoke-Pogis and Thomas Gray — At the Grave of Coleridge — On Barnet Battle-field — A Glimpse of Canterbury — The Shrines of Warwickshire — A Borrower of the Night.

A List of Books Published by

THE HOLIDAY BOOK OF THE SEASON.

SCOTT'S THE LAY OF THE LAST MINSTREL. An entirely new edition of this famous and popular poem, from *new plates*, with nearly *one hundred* new illustrations by leading American artists. Elegantly and appropriately bound, with full gilt edges. In box. Cloth, $6.00; padded calf, tree-calf, or antique morocco, $10.00. A few copies in crushed Levant, with silk linings, $25.00.

"The Lay of the Last Minstrel" is larger than its predecessors, the Holiday volumes published under Mr. Anthony's supervision, and its broad and handsome pages offer very favorable opportunities for the display of the illustrations, which are masterpieces of modern engraving.

The immediate and permanent success of "The Lady of the Lake," "Marmion," etc., has encouraged the publishers to bring out this not less popular and famous poem. It is produced in the same style, and with the same careful and elaborate style of illustration, regardless of cost, while Mr. Anthony's skilful supervision is sufficient guarantee that the work is elegant and tasteful as well as correct. The publishers feel assured that the work in its new and beautiful shape will be the **Leading Holiday Book of the Year.**

THE PETERKIN PAPERS. By LUCRETIA P. HALE. New Holiday edition, revised and enlarged, uniform with "Davy and the Goblin." Square 4to. Illustrated with a great number of new pictures. $1.50.

The continued popularity of these inimitable stories has compelled the issue of this new and enlarged edition, with new illustrations and type. "The Lady from Philadelphia," "Agamemnon," "Solomon John," and other characters of these stories have become household words in thousands of American families; and the publication of a worthy and comely edition of so delightful a classic will be hailed with joy by many old friends and new.

MURAL PAINTING. By FREDERIC CROWNINSHIELD. 1 vol. Square 8vo. With numerous diagrams and full-page illustrations. $3.00.

This series of papers has excited great interest and attention in "The American Architect;" and in its present enlarged and amended form, with many new illustrations, is still more valuable.

THE VIRGINIA CAMPAIGN OF GENERAL POPE IN 1862. Being Volume II. of Papers read before the Military Historical Society of Massachusetts. With Maps and Plans. 1 vol. 8vo. $3.00.

A careful and dispassionate account of the great retreat from the Rapidan to the Potomac, with the stories of its terrible battles, prepared by prominent military officers, and dealing with the Second Bull-Run campaign, the Fitz-John Porter affair, and other interesting matters.

SONGS AND SATIRES. A volume of poems. By JAMES JEFFREY ROCHE. 1 vol. 12mo. $1.00.

The range and versatility of these poems add to their other attractions, and make the volume a very popular one. Mr. Roche's *vers de société*, printed in "Life," and other publications, are of singular delicacy and originality, and the best of them are incorporated in this volume, together with many heretofore unpublished poems.

GENIUS IN SUNSHINE AND IN SHADOW. By M. M. BALLOU, author of "Edge-tools of Speech." 1 vol. 12mo. $1.50.

Mr. Ballou has for many years been known as one of the most industrious, accurate, and entertaining of American scholars. The present volume (his latest work) is a peculiarly interesting one, full of anecdotes and *memorabilia*, which set forth the intimate inner lives of the world's heroes and notables. They have been gathered from the most recondite sources, and skilfully massed in attractive array, forming a great collection, that is at once valuable and interesting.

Ticknor and Company.

IN OCTOBER.
A WONDERFUL WORK OF ART.
Mrs. Browning's Love Sonnets.

SONNETS FROM THE PORTUGUESE. By ELIZABETH BARRETT BROWNING. Illustrated by LUDVIG SANDÖE IPSEN 1 vol. Oblong folio (pages 13 × 16 inches), beautifully bound, gilt top. $15.00.

This magnificent work has been a labor of love for years with the artist, who is the prince of decorators, and has lavished upon it all the resources of his imagination and skill. The result is a magnificent monument to the poems that are enshrined therein, and a series of designs, the equals of which as a mere treasury of decoration and invention, apart from their significance in illustrating the immortal verse of Mrs. Browning, have never been issued in America. Each sonnet is prefaced by a richly ornamental half-title, on a full page, and is surrounded by a handsome border, emblematic in its design and composition. Mr. Ipsen has for many years been recognized as the foremost leader of art-decoration for books, both inside and outside, and has set more fashions for imitation than any other artist. This book is his crowning work, and will afford an inexhaustible treasury of decoration for students of art, and a life-study for all lovers of beauty and symmetry. Mrs. Browning's sonnets are among the noblest productions of ancient or modern literature; and their literary excellence and incomparable beauty of diction insure for them certain immortality.

RECOLLECTIONS OF EMINENT MEN, and Other Papers. By EDWIN PERCY WHIPPLE. 1 vol. Crown 8vo. With new steel portrait of the author, and preceded by the Memorial Address delivered by the Rev. Dr. C. A. BARTOL. $1.50.

A new book by Mr. Whipple is a literary event; and so many years have elapsed since his last publication, that the interest will be more intense in the present volume, which contains some of his most charming and characteristic papers, including monographs on Sumner, Motley, Agassiz, Choate, and George Eliot.

STORIES OF ART AND ARTISTS. By CLARA ERSKINE CLEMENT. 1 vol. 8vo. Profusely Illustrated. In cloth, $4.00; in half parchment, $4.50.

This work, historical and descriptive, gives a complete résumé of the History of Art, with accounts of the various schools, sketches, and anecdotes of all the great artists, with portraits and reproductions of their works. The author is well known as a charming writer and an acknowledged authority on art criticism and history.

PERSIA AND THE PERSIANS. By Hon. S. G. W. BENJAMIN, late U. S. Minister to the Court of Persia. 1 vol. 8vo. With portrait and many illustrations. Beautifully bound. $5.00. Half calf, $9.00.

The author is, perhaps, the best living authority on Persia, and this book embodies the results of his observation and experience during the years of his residence as United States Minister, combining novel and entertaining adventures and descriptions, with political and other observations of great value. His rare skill as a landscape painter has availed to give many choice pictures of the great Asiatic realm, with its stores of poetry and legend, its strange customs, and its romantic scenery and architecture.

A List of Books Published by

STEADFAST. A Novel. By ROSE TERRY COOKE, author of "Somebody's Neighbors." 1 vol. 12mo. $1.50.

Arlo Bates writes as follows, in the *Boston Courier*: "A correspondent, signing herself X, writes to the *Advertiser* in an absurd panic, lest, 'in honoring Mrs. Rose Terry Cooke, we shall, as in Hawthorne's case, wait until *Old* England tells *New* England what a genius she is neglecting.' As it has for years been generally recognized and heartily acknowledged that Mrs. Cooke has written the best stories of New-England country-life ever published, the fear of 'X' seems somewhat needless."

CONFESSIONS AND CRITICISMS. By JULIAN HAWTHORNE. 1 vol. 12mo.

A series of very delightful essays and papers, with reminiscences and other memorable papers, prepared by one of the most skilful and interesting of American authors, and calculated to attract and keep the attention of all readers. It includes a great variety of valuable miscellany, and several papers that have already become classic among people of cultivation and acumen.

THE HOUSE AT HIGH BRIDGE. By EDGAR FAWCETT. 1 vol. 12mo. $1.50.

The announcement of an entirely new novel from the pen of the writer of "Adventures of a Widow," etc., is sufficient to pique the curiosity of many readers, who find in this author the best traits of modern literature. "The House at High Bridge" is an entirely new work, not having been published serially.

FOR LATER ISSUE.

YE OLDEN TIME SERIES. The following are forthcoming volumes: —

"Literary Curiosities."

"New-England Music in the 18th and in the beginning of the 19th Century."

"Travel in Old Times, with Some Account of Stages, Taverns," etc.

"Curiosities of Politics, among the Old Federalists and Republicans."

NORA PERRY'S POEMS.

A new volume of poems by Nora Perry is now in press, and its publication will be awaited with great interest by the thousands of admirers of this brilliant and piquant writer.

A new edition of "Her Lover's Friend" and "After the Ball" (two volumes in one) is now in press.

RANKELL'S REMAINS. A Novel. By BARRETT WENDELL, author of "The Duchess Emilia." 1 vol. 12mo.

The remarkable success of Barrett Wendell's "The Duchess Emilia," a romance of the Colonna family in papal Rome, gives the best reason to hope for a similar (or even greater) triumph for his new novel, on which he has been engaged for two years. That it will be a strong and original work, no one who has read Wendell's previous story can for a moment doubt.

Ticknor and Company.

A MURAMASA BLADE. A Story of Feudalism in Old Japan. By LOUIS WERTHEIMBER. 1 vol. 8vo. Beautifully illustrated by Japanese artists. $3.00.

Mr. Wertheimber, of a scholarly Austrian family, went to Japan about the year 1870, and spent many years there, in the service of the Japanese Government. He was an extensive traveller among the inland districts and villages; and contributed many articles and series to the *Japan Mail*, and other publications. The present book is a romance of the sword, full of charming local color, true to life as it is in Japan, and full of deep and enchaining interest. Its mechanical make-up is sumptuous in every respect.

AGNES SURRIAGE. A Novel. By EDWIN LASSETTER BYNNER, author of "Damen's Ghost," "Penelope's Suitors," etc. $1.50.

This new novel by the author of "Tritons" and "Nimport" will have a large constituency of readers and admirers.

SELF-CONSCIOUSNESS OF NOTED PERSONS. By Hon. J. S. MORRILL. $1.50.

The well-known and erudite Senator from Vermont has, in this work, condensed the fruits of years of curious research in a strange and unfamiliar field. The result is a rarely entertaining volume of great value to all scholars and public men, and interesting to all readers. A small edition was privately printed some time since, and met with such praise and appreciation that Senator Morrill has since carefully revised and materially augmented it for publication.

THE MINISTER'S CHARGE. By W. D. HOWELLS, author of "The Rise of Silas Lapham," "Indian Summer," etc. $1.50.

"In this great novel of the people Henry James finds that Mr. Howells touches high-water mark; and sees an important and valuable work in this minute and subtle registering of the heavy-witted countryman's slow development under city conditions. However that may be, Howells's pure, inimitable fun is enough to carry any story he may write. Like all true fun, this has a most searching pathos all the time just at hand; and never is the real dignity of character of this actual Yankee forgotten or trifled with." — *Boston Transcript.*

STORIES AND SKETCHES. By JOHN BOYLE O'REILLY, editor of the *Pilot*, author of "Moondyne," etc. 12mo. $1.50.

The great popularity of the author, and the intrinsic merit and interest of his writings, will insure a warm reception to this collection of his latest and best works.

SAFE BUILDING. By LOUIS DE COPPET BERG. 1 vol. Square 8vo. $5.00.

A List of Books Published by Ticknor & Co.

THE MEMORIAL HISTORY OF BOSTON,

In Four Volumes. Quarto.

With more than 500 Illustrations by famous artists and engravers, all made for this work.

Edited by JUSTIN WINSOR, LIBRARIAN OF HARVARD UNIVERSITY.

Among the contributors are: —

Gov. JOHN D. LONG,
Hon. CHARLES FRANCIS ADAMS,
Rev. PHILLIPS BROOKS, D.D.,
Rev. E. E. HALE, D.D.,
Hon. ROBERT C. WINTHROP,
Hon. J. HAMMOND TRUMBULL,
Admiral G. H. PREBLE,

Dr. O. W. HOLMES,
JOHN G. WHITTIER,
Rev. J F. CLARKE, D.D.,
Rev. A. P. PEABODY, D.D.,
Col. T. W. HIGGINSON,
Professor ASA GRAY,
Gen. F. W. PALFREY,

HENRY CABOT LODGE.

VOLUME I. treats of the Geology, Fauna, and Flora; the Voyages and Maps of the Northmen, Italians, Captain John Smith, and the Plymouth Settlers; the Massachusetts Company, Puritanism, and the Aborigines; the Literature, Life, and Chief Families of the Colonial Period.

VOL. II. treats of the Royal Governors; French and Indian Wars; Witches and Pirates; The Religion, Literature, Customs, and Chief Families of the Provincial Period.

VOL. III. treats of the Revolutionary Period and the Conflict around Boston; and the Statesmen, Sailors, and Soldiers, the Topography, Literature, and Life of Boston during that time; and also of the Last Hundred Years' History, the War of 1812, Abolitionism, and the Press.

VOL IV. treats of the Social Life, Topography, and Landmarks, Industries, Commerce, Railroads, and Financial History of this Century in Boston; with Monographic Chapters on Boston's Libraries, Women, Science, Art, Music, Philosophy, Architecture, Charities, etc.

*** *Sold by subscription only. Send for a Prospectus to the Publishers,*

TICKNOR AND COMPANY, Boston.

POETS AND PROBLEMS.

By GEORGE WILLIS COOKE, author of "Ralph Waldo Emerson: His Life, Writings, and Philosophy," and "George Eliot: A Critical Study of Her Life, Writings, and Philosophy." 12mo. $2.00.

"Exceptionally fine; of critical value and full of suggestive insight." — *Traveller.*

An interesting study of the three foremost Englishmen in the republic of letters, — Tennyson, Browning, and Ruskin, — with their personal traits, literary histories, and most notable works.

EVERY-DAY RELIGION.

By JAMES FREEMAN CLARKE, D.D. $1.50.

"Full of the richest and most helpful thought." — *Boston Courier.*

"There is not a dull page in the book. Every sentence throbs with life." — *Buffalo Christian Advocate.*

EDGE-TOOLS OF SPEECH.

By MATURIN M. BALLOU. 8vo. $3.50.

"Truly 'a book which hath been culled from the flowers of all books,' including striking passages, pungent apothegms, brilliant thoughts, etc., from the great men of all ages. Every writer and speaker, professional man and student, should own this vast treasury of genius."

THE LIFE AND GENIUS OF GOETHE.

The Lectures at the Concord School of Philosophy for 1885. Edited by F. B. SANBORN and W. T. HARRIS. 1 vol. 12mo. With two portraits. $2.00.

Goethe's Youth, Self-Culture, Titanism, Märchen, Elective Affinities, Women, Faust, Portrayal of Child-Life, Schiller, Relations to English Literature, etc.

LIGHT ON THE HIDDEN WAY.

With Introduction by JAMES FREEMAN CLARKE. $1.00.

A remarkable and vivid study of immortality. All readers of literature of the supernatural, in books like "The Little Pilgrim," will be interested.

"Singularly interesting." — *Church Press.*

Sold by booksellers. Sent, postpaid, on receipt of price by the publishers,

TICKNOR AND COMPANY, Boston.

THE FAMILIAR LETTERS

OF

Peppermint Perkins.

16mo, Illustrated.

$1.00. In paper covers, 50 cents.

"These letters have attracted much attention in many quarters, and the orders for them have come in in large numbers from every State in the Union. They are original, bright, and breezy, and seem to strike a familiar chord everywhere." — *Boston Gazette.*

"A series of papers touching pretty sharply (and very funnily withal) upon fashion, society customs, personal frivolity, and ridiculous pretensions generally. These are addressed to her friend, 'Poesie Plympton' (who is abroad) in a spirit of most charming abandon, revealing such a familiarity with the scenes and subjects that she writes about that no one can doubt she has been among them taking notes, while her style indicates her femininity, though there are many who doubt it. There has nothing more piquant, spicy, and unconventional ever been published in Boston, and Peppermint 'takes the cake.'" — *Hartford Post.*

"These letters attracted not a little attention at the Hub for their audacity in kicking over the classic styles and violating all the established dogmas of dignity and lofty intellectuality. They are a reaction from the strain and intensity of ordinary Boston life, and thus supply a clearly defined want. This explains their local popularity, and gives, also, a reason why the outside world should turn the pages of the book as a sort of mirror reflecting a phase of Boston culture. It purports to be written by a woman, but there are indications that the character is assumed." — *New York Home Journal.*

"This bright series of amusing comments on characteristic failings of the last decade ... are supposed to be the weekly budgets of news written by a young girl in Boston to a dear friend in Venice. ... 'Emergency lectures,' fashionable religion, amateur cooking, horse-car politeness, servants, summer hotels, symphony concerts, and other Boston topics are wittily touched upon, and the frailty of human nature, especially of feminine human nature, is most mercilessly exposed in the various phases which they suggest." — *The Commercial Bulletin.*

TICKNOR AND COMPANY,
BOSTON.

AMERICAN GUIDE-BOOKS.

The best companions of all who wish to get the largest possible amount of pleasure out of a summer journey. The history, poetry, and legends of each locality. Scores of maps and panoramas. Prices and locations of hotels, summer resorts, and routes. Newly revised. 400 to 500 pages each. $1.50 each.

"The Osgood Guide-books are much the best we have ever had in this country, and they can challenge comparison with Baedeker's, which is the best in Europe, The volume devoted to the White Mountains is full, precise, compact, sensible, and honest." — *New York Tribune.*

NEW ENGLAND.

A guide to its cities and resorts, scenery and history. With 16 maps and plans. $1.50.

"It is a faithful, painstaking piece of work, and condenses into brief compass a vast amount of information, which all tourists to the summer resorts of New England will gladly possess." — *New York Evening Post.*

THE WHITE MOUNTAINS.

450 pages; 6 maps and 6 panoramas. $1.50.

"As perfect a thing of its kind as could well be produced. It is simply indispensable to all who visit or sojourn among the White Mountains." — *Congregationalist.*

THE MARITIME PROVINCES.

Nova Scotia, Cape Breton, New Brunswick, Prince Edward Island, Newfoundland, and Labrador. With 8 maps and plans. $1.50.

"By its intrinsic value, copiousness of information, and impartiality, it is likely to take the place of all other guides to Canada which we know of." — *Quebec Chronicle.*

THE SAUNTERER.

By CHARLES GOODRICH WHITING. Illustrated. $1.25.

"A book of unusual quality and charm. Mr. Whiting is a born poet, whose prose is often as distinctly and delightfully poetic as his verse. He is a born nature lover; few young literary men know our New England woods, pastures, hills, and rivers so intimately, in all weathers and under all skies, or have written of them so well." — *Hartford Courant.*

THE STORIED SEA.

By MRS. GEN. LEW WALLACE. $1.00.

"This airily graceful little book carries within it something of the salt sweetness of the sea, of the fantastic glow of the Orient, and the cool beauty of classic shores." — *New York Tribune.*

NANTUCKET SCRAPS.

By MRS. JANE G. AUSTIN. $1.50.

OVER THE BORDER.

By MISS E. B. CHASE. With Nova Scotia Views and Map. $1.50.

TICKNOR AND COMPANY, Boston.

THE CHOICEST NOVELS.

The Story of Margaret Kent. By Henry Hayes . $1.50
The Prelate. By Isaac Henderson 1.50
Next Door. By Clara Louise Burnham 1.50
Dr. Sevier. By George W. Cable 1.50
For a Woman. By Nora Perry 1.00
Eustis. By Robert Apthorp Boit 1.50
A Woman of Honor. By H. C. Bunner 1.25
Aubert Dubayet. By Chas. Gayarré 2.00
John Rantoul. By Henry Loomis Nelson 1.50
The Duchess Emilia. By Barrett Wendell 1.50
Daisy Miller. By Henry James 1.50
A Reverend Idol 1.50
Where the Battle was Fought. By Charles Egbert Craddock 1.50
The Led-Horse Claim. By Mary Hallock Foote . . 1.25
Miss Ludington's Sister. By Edward Bellamy . . . 1.25
Eleanor Maitland. By Clara Erskine Clement . . . 1.25
A Washington Winter. By Madeleine Vinton Dahlgren 1.50
Her Washington Season. By Jeanie Gould Lincoln . 1.50
His Two Wives. By Mary Clemmer 1.50
Dr. Grimshawe's Secret. By Nathaniel Hawthorne . . 1.50
A Midsummer Madness. By Ellen Olney Kirk . . . 1.25
The Lost Name. By Madeleine Vinton Dahlgren . . 1.00

HENRY JAMES'S

The Siege of London . . . $1.50
The Author of Beltraffio . . 1.50
Tales of Three Cities . . . 1.50

ROSE TERRY COOKE'S

The Sphinx's Children . . $1.50
Somebody's Neighbors . . . 1.50

EDMUND QUINCY'S

Wensley $1.50
The Haunted Adjutant . . 1.50

NORA PERRY'S

Book of Love Stories . . $1.00

MR. HOWELLS'S NOVELS.

Indian Summer $1.50
The Rise of Silas Lapham . 1.50
A Woman's Reason . . . 1.50
A Modern Instance 1.50
Dr. Breen's Practice . . . 1.50
A Fearful Responsibility . . 1.50

JULIAN HAWTHORNE'S

Love — or a Name $1.50
Fortune's Fool 1.50
Beatrix Randolph 1.50

EDGAR FAWCETT'S

Tinkling Cymbals $1.50
Adventures of a Widow . . 1.50
Social Silhouettes 1.50

ROBERT GRANT'S

Confessions of a Frivolous Girl $1.25
An Average Man 1.50
The Knave of Hearts . . . 1.25

EDWARD KING'S

The Golden Spike $1.50
The Gentle Savage 2.00

E. W. HOWE'S

A Moonlight Boy $1.50
The Story of a Country Town 1.50
The Mystery of the Locks . 1.50

BLANCHE W. HOWARD'S

Guenn $1.50
Aulnay Tower 1.50
Aunt Serena 1.25

HENRY GREVILLE'S

Dosia's Daughter $1.25
Cleopatra 1.25

For sale by all booksellers. Sent, postpaid, on receipt of the price, by the publishers,

TICKNOR AND COMPANY, Boston.

www.ingramcontent.com/pod-product-compliance
Lightning Source LLC
Chambersburg PA
CBHW020230240426
43672CB00006B/477